Don't Take the Bait to Escalate

"Conflict is difficult, and most of us avoid it. But what if conflict could become life-giving and good? This book offers very practical help that can help you thrive through difficult relationships and conversations."

 —**Christopher D. Hudson**, author of *100 Names of God*

"It's not hyperbole to say that *Don't Take the Bait to Escalate* is a gift to the planet. It's a masterclass in how to approach conflict with empathy, grace, kindness…and ultimately, wisdom. Wow!"

 —**Bryan Mattimore**, author of *21 Days to a Big Idea*

"In a social media age where conflict isolates and divides, Jay Payleitner brings a necessary, practical book to help us learn to see conflict as an opportunity to get closer instead of further away. Highly recommended!"

 —**Britt Mooney**, church-planting pastor and author of *Say Yes: How God-Sized Dreams Take Flight*

"Our divided society has forgotten that it's okay to agree to disagree. Jay's book is full of optimism and excellent practices we can and should (or must) all start applying to our day-to-day encounters. Thank you, Jay, for this timely advice written in plain language. Your book makes this world a better place."

 —**Mariana Ferrari**, named Top 200 most creative minds in the world, advisor to Fortune 500 CEOs, and president of DOOIT

"I love the old joke, 'I'm great at conflict, just ask any of my former friends.' As someone who chooses the jerk option far too often, I appreciate the simple way Jay shares his wisdom and the biblical foundations he applies to approaching conflicts of every stripe. Don't skim this book—allow the patterns and principles to shift your approach. Your former friends will thank you."

—**Matt Guevara**, founder of Venn Digital Marketing

"Jay Payleitner did it again. This time he took the bait to deescalate and wrote a beatitudinal book on conflict resolution. It's a timely must-read packed with timeless wisdom and embellished by the unique Payleitner wit that actually makes it fun to resolve and even prevent conflict!"

—**Maurits van Sambeek**, metaphysician from the Netherlands

"None of us can get through life without conflict—sometimes we can't even get through a day or a week without it. With his trademark humor and wit, Jay Payleitner provides an abundance of wisdom, helpful examples, timely tips, and wily tricks to successfully handle conflict in our lives."

—**Julie Bryant**, senior writer at Masterworks in Poulsbo, Washington

"*Don't Take the Bait to Escalate* is sorely needed in our anger-centric culture! It's chock-full of practical tips and fun anecdotes. Buy one for you and one for that irritating relative!"

—**Kent Evans**, executive director of Manhood Journey and author of *Wise Guys* and *The Manhood Journey*

"Powerful and timely! These truths are needed in the school-house, White House, and at your house! Payleitner offers a better way to negotiate and deal with conflict that can change every relationship for the better—it can make our country better too. Please read, apply, and share this book!"

—**David Horsager**, bestselling author of *The Trust Edge* and a leading global expert in building high-trust leaders and organizations

"I've been a jerk. Maybe you have been too. And it's likely that we've all been on the 'receiving end'—the result of someone else being a jerk in a conflict situation. Payleitner delivers a treasure trove of scenarios, illustrations, biblical insight, strategies, and applications (generally, a SOP manual) for successfully navigating through conflict."

—**Steve Hefta**, strategic account manager at Marketplace Chaplains

"Reading a Jay Payleitner book is like having a conversation with a good friend. Jay can take something serious like conflict resolution, ground it in the Bible, and then add humor and plain English to make it palatable and easy to grasp."

—**Bernard J. Forster**, hearing officer at education management consulting

"Conflict is inevitable on this side of Heaven. But we can find joy in our friendships and experience peace with the people around us. Jay Payleitner's book reveals what God has to say about resolving conflict biblically."

—**Scott LaPierre**, pastor, author, and speaker

"*Don't Take the Bait to Escalate* provides strategies to avoid taking a conflict from smoldering coals to full-scale dumpster fire. Payleitner not only offers important tactics to use (and, just as importantly, to avoid), but his wonderful anecdotes breathe life into each approach. With such a variety of tools in my conflict toolbox, I can win every conflict I engage in—and my adversary will too by ensuring the conflict bears fruit for all."

—**Brad Barbera,** innovation strategist and author of *Keep Innovation Simple: Lead with Clarity and Focus in a World of Constant Change*

"Taking a bold and honest, yet truthful and compassionate approach, Jay Payleitner dives head-first into the delicate topic of conflict. This book will equip you for any difficult conversations or negotiation and is a must-read for all."

—**Matt Haviland,** Men's Center director at Alpha Grand Rapids

"Jay Payleitner's *Don't Take the Bait to Escalate* is a well-written, superb, easy-to-read book that clearly lays out how to manage conflict and stressful situations. With case examples that strikingly illustrate his points and a step-by-step approach for assessing and managing relational issues, it is a must-read for anyone who wants to better solve conflicts, and it should become a go-to manual for therapists and psychologists."

—**Leroy R. Hall,** licensed clinical psychologist and clinical neuropsychologist

Don't Take the Bait to Escalate

Don't Take the Bait to Escalate

Conflict Is Inevitable.
Being a Jerk Is Optional.

Jay Payleitner

SALEM
BOOKS

an imprint of Regnery Publishing
Washington, D.C.

Salem Books™ is a trademark of Salem Communications Holding Corporation.
Regnery® is a registered trademark and its colophon is a trademark of Salem Communications Holding Corporation.

ISBN: 978-1-68451-187-7
eISBN: 978-1-68451-288-1

Library of Congress Control Number: 2021946358

Published in the United States by
Salem Books
An Imprint of Regnery Publishing
A Division of Salem Media Group
Washington, D.C.
www.SalemBooks.com

Manufactured in the United States of America

10 9 8 7 6 5 4 3 2 1

Books are available in quantity for promotional or premium use. For information on discounts and terms, please visit our website: www.SalemBooks.com.

To Mike Penny,
a friend and mentor who
sees the best in everyone.
Even me.

CONTENTS

CHAPTER 7
TACTICS AND TRICKS

CHAPTER 8
A WAY OF LIFE   173

CONFLICT IN LIFE IS INEVITABLE

Congratulations. You're a member of the human race with a sincere desire to play nice with all the other members of the human race. That's an excellent goal. Getting along with others increases your chances of making friends, making money, finding romance, living in harmony, sharing your faith, and doing other stuff you want to do.

Unfortunately, sometimes playing nice is not so easy. Most of us know people who could use a punch in the face. Right? Well please don't. It would bloody your knuckles and the situation probably wouldn't improve, anyway. Besides, for the most part, Christians should be looking for peaceful solutions to our differences of opinion. Not by being wimps or avoiding debates, but by doing our best to not stir up trouble. Romans 12:18 doesn't exactly forbid using physical engagement, but its instruction is fairly clear, "If possible, so far as it depends on you, be at peace with all people" (NASB).

So with whom might you not be living in peace? The list of possibilities is endless. Any situation in which you come into connection with others—face-to-face or otherwise—opens the door to conflict.

- Family
- Work
- Friends
- Neighbors
- Church members
- Social media
- Video conferencing
- Politics and government
- Teachers and coaches
- Plumbers, electricians, and auto mechanics
- Salesclerks, Uber drivers, and waitstaff
- People who need to know Jesus
- God

The list could be longer, but you get the point. Conflict is here or coming soon. The Bible confirms, "In this world you will have trouble" (John 16:33). That truth is more than a warning; it's a reminder to get ready.

NO TWO CONFLICTS ARE ALIKE

Along with this inevitability comes the realization that conflicts have a range of intensities and longevities. Some conflicts are life and death. Most are not.

Getting cut off in traffic can be intense, but it doesn't last long. That is, unless you are overtaken by a sudden urge to escalate the situation, follow that driver home, and deliver vengeance.

Squabbles with neighbors can pop up unexpectedly and then subside with the seasons. A few friendly waves and small talk about the weather may be all it takes to ease any tension.

On the job, a minor misunderstanding with the friendly guy who works down the hallway can be settled over a cold beverage. But when a new boss comes in and starts making massive changes, you may need to summon great wisdom and patience to de-escalate that conflict.

I think we all have one person in our lives who began as a mild irritation but morphed into a severely destructive buffoon. Don't you wish you had dealt with that troublemaker's bad attitude early on?

Family may be the most prevalent source of conflict. Just about everyone has memories of one, two, or twenty uncomfortable Thanksgiving gatherings. It could be the result of one individual at the table who simply had a rough year. Or it could be some kind of feud simmering for decades that finally boils over when someone says, "Please pass the stuffing."

Marriage and parenthood bring their own guaranteed conflicts. The good news is that—perhaps as part of God's design—a conflict with your spouse or kids can actually leave your family with a closer bond. Ask any long-married couple and they'll recall the time they "hit bottom" as a turbulent season that ultimately made their marriage stronger.

Friendships are often *built* on conflict as individuals find themselves vying for recognition in academic pursuits, on sports teams, or on the job with people of similar age, interests, and abilities. Those friendships strengthen as a result of differences of opinion, verbal sparring, and the occasional squabble. Intuitively we know that "iron sharpens iron" (Proverbs 27:17).

Any conflict you might be having with God can also be a good thing. He certainly can handle it and knows what's going on in your life. There's nothing you can think, do, or say that will cause God to love you less or that will derail His purpose for your life.

CONFLICT AFTERMATH

So, conflicts come in all relationships, in a variety of shapes and sizes. Minor annoyances or differences of opinions can be easily brushed off or fade away on their own. But major clashes can impact every facet of our lives. Like a gargoyle squatting on your nightstand, a contentious conflict can conclude your days with distress, haunt your dreams, and still be there in the morning. There's no doubt: conflicts that continually drag you down need to be faced with candor, intentionality, and wisdom.

As we've already confirmed, a healthy, well-managed conflict can be a good thing. When the dust settles you can be left with new insights, new friends, and new purpose. There are even occasions when a nasty, frustrating conflict can be flipped into a win-win scenario. But that rarely happens by accident.

Very often, the resolution of a conflict will only come through some kind of negotiation. Which is why you'll find that word— "negotiation"—come up often in the chapters to follow. At any given time, you could find yourself in formal arbitration or informal bargaining over an enormous financial expenditure, ownership of some piece of property, parental visitation rights, the cost of roof repair, the dimensions of your cubicle, thermostat settings, wall-paper samples, or pizza toppings.

Negotiation is how your teenager gets a later curfew. Negotiation is how automakers and unions stay in business. Negotiation is how toddlers learn to share their beach toys. Negotiation is how America's Founding Fathers set up Congress so that small states and big states would be fairly represented.

You might think that simply declaring "My way or the highway" is the best way to solve any conflict. But you would be wrong.

For the most part, you want to be thoughtful and even empathetic when it comes to conflicts. If possible, you'll want to get ahead of encounters and clashes before they get ugly. If you see one coming, you'll want to prepare your heart and mind to respond. Proverbs 22:3 recommends, "A prudent person foresees danger and takes precautions. The simpleton goes blindly on and suffers the consequences" (NLT).

But what about that conflict coming around the corner that takes you by complete surprise? Good news. There are strategies you can put in place now that will allow you to face unexpected conflicts with clarity, common sense, and wisdom.

You picked up this book because a conflict has crept into your life or you are anticipating one in the near future, and you want to handle it constructively. Or maybe you're trying to help someone you care about deal with a difficult dose of conflict.

In the chapters ahead, you'll discover more than twenty different situational conflicts that were resolved triumphantly, a dozen or so skills you may want to polish before your next negotiation, and another dozen slightly sneaky tactics to keep handy just in case.

Before that we have some myths to debunk, some definitions to clarify, four critical factors to consider, and three mistakes to avoid as you consider your response to any conflict.

CHAPTER 1

THE CONFLICT CONUNDRUM

Studies of human response to conflict are, shall we say, inconclusive. Experts often try to tuck adversarial encounters into one of the neat little boxes labeled "task conflict," "relationship conflict," "value conflict," or "legal conflict." But conflict is rarely that simple. Also, people generally assume that conflict is bad news, but that's a pessimistic view of human relationships.

Ironically, strategies for resolving conflict actually conflict with each other. Should adversaries communicate openly and reveal their emotions? Or leave any and all emotions off the table?

Those who have suffered workplace or relational setbacks because of discord might conclude there's nothing redeemable about conflict. You might agree. After all, it seems like the Bible puts a significant emphasis on *avoiding* conflict.

Don't have anything to do with foolish and stupid arguments, because you know they produce quarrels. And the Lord's servant must not be quarrelsome but must be kind to everyone, able to teach, not resentful. (2 Timothy 2:23–24)

Avoid foolish controversies and genealogies and arguments and quarrels about the law, because these are unprofitable and useless. Warn a divisive person once, and then warn them a second time. After that, have nothing to do with them. You may be sure that such people are warped and sinful; they are self-condemned. (Titus 3:9–11)

Better to live in a desert than with a quarrelsome and nagging wife. (Proverbs 21:19)

A closer look at these and other passages reveals that, rather than condemning all conflict, Scripture is actually identifying the kinds of argument to avoid. That is, we should avoid arguments that are foolish, unkind, resentful, or hinder teaching.

The passage above from Titus warns us to avoid unprofitable conflict and not to boast about the spiritual pedigree of our family tree. Also, don't nitpick Levitical law. In addition, it's permissible to give troublemakers one or two warnings, but if they continue to incite conflict, they condemn themselves as warped and sinful; therefore, "have nothing to do with them."

The verse from Proverbs 21 wisely suggests a husband refrain from turning his wife into a shrew. (You didn't want to live in the desert anyway, right?)

THE SOURCE OF CONFLICT

Turning to another passage from the Bible, we get an even more complete understanding of the *source* of conflict. James tells us to beware the desires of the world. We pursue material possessions, status, money, and influence. God isn't surprised by that; He understands the temptations of the temporary world and how they lead to conflict. He also provides a way out: just ask God for what you really need. But even that comes with a warning: we need to make our requests to God *with the right motives*.

> What causes fights and quarrels among you? Don't they come from your desires that battle within you? You desire but do not have, so you kill. You covet but you cannot get what you want, so you quarrel and fight. You do not have because you do not ask God. When you ask, you do not receive, because you ask with wrong motives, that you may spend what you get on your pleasures. (James 4:1–3)

When conflict shows up—and it will—how should we respond? Clearly we need a plan. Conflict crops up in ways large and small. Destructive and instructive. Between people who genuinely love each other and between perfect strangers. Between faithful believers and those who do not yet know the Savior.

In other words, there's a lot riding on the challenge in front of us. Conflict can derail friendships, marriages, and our ability to share our faith. Not to mention the inevitable conflicts we all face in our careers and business alliances.

Money should never be the deciding factor in your biggest life decisions, but unresolved conflict often has an impact on your wallet. The most obvious examples are lost raises and missed promotions because you and your boss are butting heads. Distractions from belligerent or boneheaded colleagues can easily decrease your productivity. Entering a negotiation with a sales representative, we expect a bit of conflict. But does that give us permission to be a jerk?

Do you manage or run your own company? Then you know how conflict with outside entities—customers, suppliers, competitors, government agencies—will impact your profitability.

Perhaps the most exasperating conflict conundrums are those experiences that come completely out of nowhere. Your lovely niece is planning her wedding and suddenly much of your family gets sucked into her bridezilla vortex. You're driving home from a nice evening out when red flashing lights appear in your rearview mirror. Walking home from school, suddenly you find yourself in a fistfight with your best friend. You and your spouse find yourselves doing battle over…peanut butter. Ahead, we'll invest a few pages on how best to deal with all of those not-so-typical problematic occurrences.

The bulk of this book will be dedicated to helping you bring resolution to strife, disputes, debates, or disharmony that have a profound and lasting impact on the parties involved. While some conflicts can be dismissed with minimal fuss, many need to be handled with care or avoided with finesse.

QUESTIONS WORTH ASKING

Before getting too far into strategies for resolving conflict, let's answer some questions about it that frequently come up.

- Will every conflict you face be resolved? *Probably not.*
- Might some conflicts best be ignored? *Indeed, but don't use that as an excuse for not dealing with the conflicts that do need your attention.*
- Are some conflicts beneficial? *Surprisingly yes.*
- Is the other person always at fault? *C'mon, you know the answer to that.*
- In business negotiations, can I be ruthless and unyielding? *That's your call, but if this is a long-term relationship or if you care about your reputation, you may want to turn it down a notch.*
- Are there any clever tactics and tricks to winning arguments and negotiations? *Certainly. See chapter 7, titled "Tactics and Tricks."*
- Are there any big secrets to conflict resolution? *Yes, they're in the last chapter. But please don't peek ahead.*

There are all kinds of questions regarding the conflicts we face as humans in this world. The one that keeps popping up—especially among Christians—concerns the responsibility we have to "turn the other cheek."

That's a tricky business. We want to be peacemakers. But the Bible seems to go beyond the idea of just promoting harmony. It appears to be suggesting we should all be pushovers when responding to conflict by giving in and backing down. For example, in the Sermon on the Mount, Jesus illustrates turning the other cheek with the example that "if someone demands your coat, offer your shirt also" (Luke 6:29 NLT). The Beatitudes promise that the meek will inherit the earth. In Titus 3:2, we're even told "to speak evil of no one, to avoid quarreling, to be gentle, and to show perfect courtesy toward all people."

That's all straight from God's Word, but for some reason it just doesn't feel right. That kind of passivity and gentleness is not a plan you might expect to find in a book on conflict resolution. It's also not an easy assignment in today's culture. Selfishness thrives. Bullies bully. Coaches expect wins. Bosses have budgets. Sales reps have quotas. Spouses have needs.

Conflict is part of everyday life.

When it comes to our financial well-being, that's especially true. We understand that we're not supposed to "love money." After all, "The love of money is a root of all kinds of evil" (1 Timothy 6:10). But money itself is not evil. It's a resource. Money is a practical tool, and we need to be smart with it. Especially if we expect to take responsibility for our own food, clothing, and shelter, and also hope to meet the biblical mandates to feed the hungry, clothe the naked, and support ministries— including our own church families.

So let's admit that conflicts will crop up as a result of our own human temptations and the demanding nature of our culture. That's not necessarily bad news if we have an effective plan in place for dealing with them. In every case, we have a responsibility to ask the question: *Do you want to escalate or de-escalate?*

The choice is yours.

LET'S USE THE TERM "ADVERSARY"

Almost a hundred times in the upcoming chapters, we need a workable generic term to describe the individual with whom you may be in conflict—a boss, spouse, neighbor, sales rep, and so on.

They're not all enemies, combatants, or bad dudes. Actually, most are people you care about. You don't want to escalate conflict because you want or need them in your life. But for the sake of our examples—most based on true stories—they are framed in an adversarial position. So, prepare yourself to see the term *adversary* in just about every chapter. Don't think of it as a pejorative term, just one that works for our purposes. Deal?

CHAPTER 2

THE FOUR FACTORS

We've already established that conflicts and potential conflicts come in all shapes and sizes. To prove the point, let's list a few:

- A teenager requests a later curfew.
- An attorney files a class-action lawsuit against a fast-food giant.
- JFK tells the Soviets they cannot harbor nuclear missiles in Cuba.
- A drunk driver backs into your car in a parking lot.
- A film actor walks off the set because his wife is in labor with twins.
- At your annual review, you make the case for a substantial raise.
- Your spouse forgets your anniversary... again.

You can easily imagine—or have experienced—a slew of other conflicts, but these seven examples should do the job helping to explain the Four Factors that need to be considered when facing any and all occurrences of conflict.

FACTOR #1: DECIDE WHAT YOU REALLY WANT

Entering into any conflict, it may seem like what you want is pretty straightforward. An 11 p.m. curfew. A billion-dollar settlement. Nukes removed. Your fender repaired. Getting to the maternity ward ASAP. A 20 percent salary bump. A nice anniversary gift from your spouse.

If the conflict ends with those outcomes, you'll be living in a magical world of blissful euphoria, right? Plus, those payoffs you have identified are all measurable. You entered the conflict with a specific objective. For all intents and purposes, the conflict should be over if and when a compromise is reached, the dollar amount is met, the threat is over, or the gift is received.

But are those straightforward objectives what you really want? Might there be emotional, relational, political, or professional needs that are equally or more important? Moreover, those categories of needs are not as easily measured, which means the successful resolution of the conflict is in question. In most cases, some additional level of mutual understanding and acceptance between adversaries in a conflict needs to be attained. Publicly or privately. Spoken or unspoken. What's more, true reconciliation of a conflict may be immediate or take years.

By digging a little deeper into personal motivations and long-term implications, we can see that "what you really want" can be multi-layered and not easy to nail down.

- That teenager does want more freedom, but he or she has an even deeper desire for parental trust and respect.
- For some attorneys, more important than the big settlement is the notoriety among their peers.
- John F. Kennedy needed the 1962 Cuban missile crisis to end peacefully with the destruction of the missile sites and removal of the nuclear warheads. Moreover, the young president needed to avoid World War III.
- A parking lot dent is easy to fix. A physical altercation with an angry, inebriated stranger has more dire consequences.
- When an actor abruptly leaves the set, the director has some immediate decisions to make. This conflict—with implications for reputations and careers—won't be resolved in the moment.
- Are you asking for a raise? A bigger office? A secure future? Or something else?
- Finally, an argument in marriage about trivial matters almost always has deeper undertones and implications. Proceed with caution.

What you really want is not always immediately obvious. If you initiated the conflict, then you probably had some time to examine that question and develop strategies to achieve your objective. Such as when a class-action lawyer meets with representatives from the injured parties and decides what settlement they would accept. Or when an underpaid brand manager sends out feelers around the industry to see what other brand managers are making. (In the process, they may discover their current compensation is actually above the average.)

Even if the actions of your adversary triggered the conflict, often you have some time to consider your next move. A president gathers the security council. A mom and dad put their heads together before responding to their teenager's request.

Of course, if your conflict takes you by surprise, there may not be time to consider what you really want. Such is the case of the fender-bender in a parking lot, the director suddenly without an actor, or any urgent predicament. In that case, let common sense prevail. See if you can make it *less urgent*. Be safe. Delay major decisions. What appears to be a path to a quick resolution may actually be a trail leading off a cliff. Haste can make a bad situation worse.

Before a scheduled or anticipated conflict, do your research. As for unscheduled conflicts, don't live as a pessimist, but do occasionally consider how you might respond to real-life situations with your upcoming events and various relationships. What if you're confronted by a mugger? What if a good friend wants you to lie for him? What if your teenage daughter reveals she's pregnant? What if you open a carton of campaign signs at the rally and your candidate's name is spelled wrong? What if a waiter spills the soup du jour in your lap?

What emotions or thought process will rule your response? Here's a hint: in all your conflicts—especially the ones that take you by surprise—see if you can channel the gifts of the Holy Spirit already at work in your life. "The fruit of the Spirit is love, joy, peace, patience, kindness, goodness, faithfulness, gentleness, self-control" (Galatians 5:22–23 NASB).

Embodying those nine character traits may help you decide what you really want.

FACTOR #2: KNOW THE RISKS

There's risk to any conflict. Obvious and not so obvious. That idea shouldn't come as a surprise. If it gets ugly, the risk is losing a longtime friend, client, or vendor. Words taken the wrong way can strain relationships in families, at the workplace, and between neighbors. Both parties may enter a conflict, negotiation, or debate in good faith expecting a fair exchange of ideas. But too often someone takes the bait to escalate. A back is turned. A door is slammed. A nasty email is sent. A button is pushed. A punch is thrown. A threat is made. Volume increases. Pride, greed, fear, or envy takes over.

Those actions and emotions can all occur within the context of sincerely trying to resolve the conflict. The repercussions can last long after. In the end—if you do get what you really want—the question may still linger. Was it worth it?

Going a step further, you may not have considered there are risks inherent even if the conflict is resolved in your favor. Let's revisit our seven examples.

- By bringing up the curfew topic, a teenager is opening the door to a longer discussion about responsibility, friends, dating, college plans, and so on. Plus, if they get that later curfew, there may be a stricter level of accountability. Heart-to-heart conversations between teens and parents are a good thing. But they take time, and they're also risky business.
- Hey, counselor. Don't forget that fast-food giant is going to hire its own powerhouse attorneys. Can you take that heat? Plus, class-action lawsuits may drag

on for years. That's good news for billings. But not-so-good news for stress levels and family time.

- President Kennedy's advisors spelled out several possible courses of action in response to the Russians' intent to install nukes in Cuba. Each had its own set of risks, with millions of lives at stake. Not sure if he had a Bible on hand, but Kennedy was probably aware of the principle set forth in Proverbs 11:14, "For lack of guidance a nation falls, but victory is won through many advisers."

- In some parking-lot altercations, it's risky even to get out of your car. Here's a good rule of thumb: never get into a fight with a guy who's had too much to drink.

- An actor leaving a set could get blacklisted. A director firing an actor risks decimating his shooting schedule and his production budget.

- That 20 percent raise you're seeking might come with new responsibilities you can't handle, a move you don't want, or a schedule you can't keep. Give your boss an ultimatum and she might call your bluff.

- It's risky bringing up your spouse's shortcomings because they will very likely bring up yours.

Knowing there are risks involved shouldn't preclude you from entering a conflict. Finding yourself in a precarious situation or in a position of authority may require you to step up and face an adversary. That might mean staring down the Russians, pleading a case in court, being firm with a teenager, speaking truth to power, or protecting your loved ones.

As a person of integrity, you may have no choice but to take a stand on issues of right and wrong. Other times, a conflict may not have moral implications, but threatens your economic well-being. Just remember there's a risk in playing hardball in financial negotiations. Trying to squeeze a few extra nickels out of a longtime client may backfire when they choose a better price over loyalty. A billing error by a supplier, lender, or landlord may induce you to withhold a payment, but that could end up damaging your credit rating. Some folks see money as a tool; others see it as a way to keep score.

Worth noting: Some conflicts have virtually no risk at all. For instance, asking the owner of a used lawnmower to knock twenty bucks off his asking price may seem contentious, but it's not at all. He can say yes or no; you can choose to buy it or not. When you ask a professor to reevaluate a grade or ask a ticket broker for a refund, you may see it as a potential conflict. But that's only if they say "no" and you respond with some kind of escalation.

Approach any conflict or potential conflict with your eyes open. Gauge a realistic appraisal of the worst-case scenario. Weigh that against the possible gain. After establishing what you want (Factor #1), decide what you are willing to risk (Factor #2).

By the way, once you recognize the short and long-term implications of risks, you'll see another good reason not to take the bait to escalate.

FACTOR #3: EMPATHIZE WITH YOUR ADVERSARY

The world could use a little more empathy. Dwelling solely on our own problems seems to be the driving force for most people today. Even more troubling, we tend to surround ourselves only with people who think exactly like we do so that our problems, opinions, and way of thinking are reaffirmed. Collectively, we whine, point fingers, wring our hands, and blame the other side—never stopping to think, *maybe they have a point?*

But enough about solving all the problems in the world. Empathy is a valuable trait that will make your own life easier. Every relationship you have will benefit.

Empathy is all about putting yourself in someone else's shoes. Seeing and understanding their perspective. Not necessarily agreeing, but acknowledging they have a right to an opinion. Like you, they need the freedom to decide what they really want and what risks they are going to take. By taking into account their objectives, you open the door to productive interaction. Empathy is the foundation of the Golden Rule, "Do to others as you would have them do to you" (Luke 6:31).

Having empathy is good advice for dealing with friends and loved ones. It's even better advice for dealing with adversaries in your next conflict. Thoughtfully considering the other side of the debate or negotiation drastically increases your chances of "winning."

Let's flip the scripts and consider the motivations and goals of the adversaries in our seven examples:

- Is it just that parents want their teenager to be safe? Nope. Mom and Dad are envisioning life two decades into the future, hoping and praying for a devoted family complete with well-adjusted grandkids and happy holidays. They fear how confrontations now can spill over into adulthood. That teenager would do well to reaffirm a sincere commitment to family and a healthy future.

- Good lawyers don't just build their own cases; they spend half their efforts considering the arguments and evidence the other side will present.
- Russian Premier Nikita Khrushchev was likely motivated by his need to balance power; in 1962, the U.S. had considerable advantage in the location and quantity of nuclear warheads. President Kennedy also knew that after the showdown in Cuba, Khrushchev had to save face and claim some kind of victory for Russia. It's also likely that both men assumed the other did not want to call for a nuclear first strike.
- When a drunk driver backs into your car, his next step is unpredictable. He could speed off recklessly into other traffic, sit behind the wheel weeping, exit his car with remorse and full cooperation, or come at you with a mouth full of curse words and a tire iron in his hand. He probably doesn't want the cops involved, but—after making sure of your own safety—calling 911 is probably your first priority. Even if the collision was your fault, you'll want an official record.
- Actors and directors are engaged in an art form, a personal investment, a partnership, and a business. Reputation seems to be paramount in Hollywood. Given the nature of filmmaking, during a conflict on set it may be impossible to know where the priority of either adversary lies.
- Many bosses simply want minimal hassles and productive employees. They have to justify their budgets, but handing out raises is one of the joys of management.

Still, maybe your boss has her own agenda, which could be vying for her own promotion, wrestling with a personal issue, or looking for a reason to fire you.

- Before attacking your spouse for forgetting your anniversary, bring it up with an attitude of partnership, curiosity, and even playfulness. You do want to uncover any underlying issues. In the meantime, study your spouse. Know his or her priorities, likes, and dislikes. Determine his or her love language. No one should know your spouse better than you.

Considering the perspective of your adversary reveals clues regarding how far to go in your own course of action or negotiation strategy. You can never really know what another person is thinking, but there are clues to be uncovered. Talk to other parents. Talk to other attorneys. Talk to other heads of state. Do your due diligence. Ask around. Who do you know who has been in a similar situation?

One option is to communicate clearly with your adversary in the conflict. Too often, we assume we know what they're thinking. Why guess if you can get them to just tell you what they want?

In many cases, being open and honest with your adversary will free them to put their own cards on the table. Later in this book, we'll explore case studies in which both parties in a negotiation openly revealed their fundamental, minimal objectives. Those examples reveal the power of straightforward communication. When both parties divulge the essentials of what they really want, more often than you might imagine a resolution is imminent.

Within families—surprise, surprise—it's often not complicated at all. The objectives are not in conflict. A teenager wants to build a comfortable future and may even confess to wanting to find a loving spouse and provide a few grandkids someday. Both husbands and wives want to laugh, snuggle, hold hands, love and respect each other, and chase dreams together.

A little empathy goes a long way.

FACTOR #4: EXPECT THE WIN

Let's explore our seven scenarios again, this time with a hint of optimism. After identifying what you really want, doing a risk assessment, and seeing the challenge from all sides, you have earned the right to expect a victorious outcome to any conflict. Hopefully, that's good news for you and your adversary.

- When a teenager asks for a bit more freedom, it's likely because they feel they've earned it. Any parent should jump at the chance to talk openly about freedom, decision-making, and responsibility. After all, in a few years that teen is going to be making all their own decisions. While they are under your roof, you want to have frequent, vibrant conversations about how that young man or woman can apply wisdom and common sense to their future. Put it all out there. Hopes, dreams, fears, expectations, and unconditional love.
- Attorneys need to enter a courtroom or conference room with confidence. Put your client first. Do your homework. Gather the best team possible. Expect the win. But don't count your settlement before it's awarded. Always remember that unfavorable rulings are also part of your career.

- History confirms there were days of tension and uncertainty during the Cuban missile crisis. The Cold War escalated in the following months. But in 1963, the Limited Nuclear Test Ban Treaty was negotiated and signed, and later the infamous "hotline" was installed, establishing a direct line of communication between Washington and Moscow to help reduce the possibility of war by miscalculation.

- It's entirely possible that the parking-lot altercation could be the best thing to happen to that unfortunate inebriated driver. Perhaps it's even a life-saving moment. If he needs help with an addiction, this might be the "hitting bottom" he needs. Being delayed by the cops in that parking lot keeps him off the road that night. Maybe he needs a friend, and that could be you. Stranger things have happened.

- If an actor abruptly leaves a set to be with his wife at the birth of their twins, that seems like a valid reason to me. Hollywood could use more professionals exhibiting devotion to family. It's possible that actor gets a reputation—not for being a liability, but as a dependable person with convictions and dedication.

- You deserve the raise. You get the raise, plus an extra week's vacation. And a corner office! (Or maybe you don't get the raise now, but you've gained some new respect from the boss. That's always a good thing.)

- Every marriage needs a few long, difficult, wonderful, heartfelt conversations. Sometimes by hitting bottom and climbing out of that pit together, your marriage becomes stronger. Sometimes a minor conflict serves

as a reminder of your wedding vows. Or maybe that
forgotten anniversary gift wasn't forgotten at all. True
story: For the first ten years of our marriage, I bought
something nice for Rita on our anniversary and she
got me just a card. It hurt a bit. After finally gener-
ating the guts to ask her why she was snubbing me
every year, the truth came out. In her family, tradition
dictated that *only* the husbands gave anniversary
gifts. Who knew? Since then, her anniversary gift
giving has improved dramatically.

Living in the light of hope is the best way to approach conflict
in the family, on the job, or just doing life, whether that conflict
sneaks up on you or you see it coming from a long way off. It doesn't
matter who started it. It doesn't matter if the solution is obvious or
infinitely complex. Expect the win. Choose to see the dawn even in
the darkness. If it helps, embrace the words of British Prime Minister
Winston Churchill, "If you're going through hell, keep going."

Certainly, there's work to do. Decisions to make. Risks to take.
Two sides to contemplate.

But if you believe in God, grace, salvation, and Jesus's imminent
return, you have the right to be optimistic. Because you know it's
all going to work out (though maybe not right away). As a matter
of fact, Christians are actually promised some difficult times in the
course of their lives. In John 16:33, Jesus offers a word of warning
and a wonderful promise, "In this world you will have trouble. But
take heart! I have overcome the world."

In general, you may want to approach every conflict with the
anticipation of a beneficial outcome. If for no other reason, conflict
proves you're not a hermit; you're out in the world interacting and

getting things done. Conflict gives all those involved new perspectives and possible new solutions. Healthy debate clarifies and strengthens your own convictions. Friendships and partnerships are forged in conflict—sometimes with your adversary!

Conflict also can provide a chance to solve a problem that has little or nothing to do with the dispute. People in conflict often have unspoken needs that, just maybe, you can help meet.

APPLYING THE FOUR FACTORS

You may not be a parent, spouse, lawyer, president, or filmmaker. But I hope seeing the Four Factors applied to our seven sample scenarios has given you insight into how to approach your own conflicts.

If it's not obvious, allow me to reaffirm some of the principles on conflict resolution we learned along the way.

- Talk it out.
- Equip yourself to slay giants.
- Stand up to threats.
- See the humanity in your adversary.
- Choose relationships over career.
- Respectfully ask for what you deserve.
- Trust love.

After the next two short chapters, we're going to look at more than twenty case studies and you'll see how the Four Factors are wisely put to use or possibly overlooked. Sometimes, it's not easy to see how all four apply. But they do.

CHAPTER 3

THE THREE MISTAKES

Whitle the Four Factors should be considered for just about every conflict, there are three common behaviors you should mostly avoid.

MISTAKE #1: CASTING BLAME

If you messed up and are fully or partially responsible for a conflict causing grief, frustration, financial hardship, or fear, I recommend you step up and take the heat. Authentic and sincere apologies are exceedingly rare. Asking forgiveness without making a ton of excuses is a powerful position to take. It may feel like accepting blame is a sign of weakness, but in most cases it's just the opposite.

Often you only see apologies in forced scenarios or publicity spins. But if you step forward quickly and take the blame, especially in a position of authority, people will be surprised and will respect you for it.

By accepting responsibility, you're displaying the virtue of honesty. You are expressing confidence that you are strong enough—as an individual, company, team, or family—to bear the burden of making things right. If the conflict is on public display, you are lifting the burden from other participants who are unsure about their own guilt or contribution to the problem. By taking the blame, you have gained the right to initiate the healing process, which will resolve the conflict more efficiently.

The benefits of accepting responsibility for a conflict are so significant that you may want to consider that option, even if the conflict is not your fault!

No matter what, don't be part of the blame game. Yes, sometimes you have to CYA (cover your assets). But if your initial instinct is to accuse and point fingers at friends and colleagues, you're not resolving anything. Onlookers will assume or recognize your culpability, and the crisis will still be on the table.

It's almost always better to fall on the grenade—to take one for the team. After taking responsibility, you can add your spin, even blaming some positive aspect of your own character.

- "It's my fault. As usual, I was trying to get a head start on the project and I moved too fast."
- "You can blame me for not being available. I had turned off my phone for some uninterrupted family time."
- "I'm sorry. It worked so well last time, I thought my luck would hold out."

You don't want to have the reputation as the king or queen of excuses. Don't go on and on with justifications and rationalizations. But remember, your alibi or excuse comes after you've accepted the burden of making things right.

If you do know who caused the conflict, feel free to take them aside and spell out the benefits of taking the blame. But, as a rule, don't be the person who throws someone else under the bus. Or worse, the person who whines, "It's not my fault."

MISTAKE #2: MAKING A SNAP DECISION

You don't always have time. But often you can *make* time.

Here's a rule of thumb: the quality of the resolution to most conflicts is markedly improved by gathering all the facts and applying careful consideration. Examples?

- Rather than assess an immediate punishment, parents need to join forces, talk things out, and come to an agreement on what sanctions or confiscations to impose on any young rulebreaker or tantrum thrower.
- Rather than key in the codes to arm the nuclear football, a U.S. president should probably think twice (or thrice) before actuating a worldwide nuclear holocaust.
- Rather than assume the worst when you see your spouse has been texting their high school sweetheart, find out whether that person is on the committee organizing the next class reunion.

Snap decisions often escalate a conflict. Better for coaches to spend a time-out. Better for purchasing agents to confirm the accuracy of that confusing quote. Better for the church elders not to rely on hearsay and gossip.

You may be surprised at how many people will say yes if you ask for time. "Can I have until the end of the day?" "I hadn't thought of that perspective, can I consider that angle and get back to you?" Things that seem like they require snap decisions often don't; you can always ask.

If you're in a position of power, you may have the authority to make a snap decision. That impulse might even end the particular conflict at hand. But don't be surprised if another rift looms right around the corner.

As you approach your next conflict, weigh these two contradictory aphorisms and then decide which is best: "He who hesitates is lost" or "Haste makes waste."

MISTAKE #3: INSISTING ON A COMPROMISE

One obvious strategy for resolving differences is to dictate a compromise. Agreeing to some kind of give-and-take may sound pretty good, but compromise can come with all kinds of frustration and false hope. Often there is no middle ground, and by insisting on some kind of happy medium you will have abandoned the search for the best option.

- He wants to live in Seattle. She wants to live in Miami. A compromise suggests they move to Wichita.
- The production house says it needs three weeks to finish the commercial. The Super Bowl is in one week.

A compromise on that production schedule means the spot—ready in two weeks—won't air and the five-million-dollar media buy loses its impact.

- When the city council votes to ban leaf burning, a neighborhood coalition demands a compromise allowing bonfires on Saturdays and Sundays. Do you really want the emergency rooms filled on weekends with kids suffering from asthma?

Compromise does have its place. When it comes to negotiating a dollar amount, go ahead and consider finding a consensus somewhere between your two numbers. Compromise can also work with the division of duties and many calendar clashes.

But sometimes the best alternative to compromise is to look for a *third option*. Which means you need to keep looking for alternatives not yet considered. Better to make a slow decision than a bad one.

Other possibilities to consider might be as simple as taking turns, bringing in additional resources, walking away, or heroically letting your adversary have their way.

Also worth noting: while a compromise can usually be revisited, the mistake of casting blame or making a snap decision can almost never be taken back.

Like so many negotiations, your approach will be different on the job, at home, in the neighborhood, or with a stranger. With people you care about, your best compromise includes a little more give and a little less take.

CHAPTER 4

THE TWO CHOICES

After embracing the Four Factors and avoiding the Three Mistakes, it's time to deliberate over your Two Choices.

TO ESCALATE

Why would you ever want to escalate a conflict? Why would someone ever pound on a boss's desk, slam a bedroom door, go on strike, or threaten divorce? Mostly because they're trying to make a point. They're trying to get the undivided attention of their adversary or the general public. From their perspective, they've tried everything else. They desperately want their needs and expectations to be taken seriously.

Escalating a conflict may feel like pouring gasoline on a fire. But when it's part of a larger strategy or some kind of collective bargaining, it can be very effective. Please remember, if escalation is ever part of your strategy, you'll want to keep a fire extinguisher handy.

In military parlance, "saber rattling" is a kind of escalation. Soviet Premier Nikita Khrushchev was brandishing a proverbial sword in 1962 when he ordered nuclear missile sites to be built in Cuba. U.S. President John F. Kennedy responded with his own threat of military force when he ordered the naval blockade of Soviet cargo ships. That bilateral escalation led to an ultimate de-escalation.

History is filled with protests, marches, rallies, sit-ins, campaigns, and demonstrations that brought attention to worthy causes—often escalating conflict for a season. Even so, Martin Luther King Jr. wisely confirmed that escalation should seek a peaceful resolution. "Man must evolve for all human conflict a method which rejects revenge, aggression, and retaliation," he said. "The foundation of such a method is love."

In a later chapter, we explore the tactics of autoworkers unions purposefully escalating the hostilities in contract negotiations. Walking out of arbitration, grandstanding for the press, and going on strike are notorious methods of negotiating for union bargaining committees.

You don't have to be a fan of escalation to admit that sometimes it works. Especially when the adversaries have military might, a growing political movement, or an organized coalition backing them up. While conflicts between organizations make headlines, it's conflicts between individuals that seem to create more personal risk.

TO DE-ESCALATE

When all the posturing, protesting, and door-slamming is over, what happens to the conflict? It's usually still there. Even worse, escalation often leaves a trail of destruction with even more baggage and a little bit of anger and loathing thrown in. In most cases—especially when you're personally invested in the outcome of the conflict—the best choice is de-escalation.

How does one do that? Keep reading. Solutions lie ahead.

In the meantime, here are a few hints about what's coming up. These proven de-escalation strategies are generously revealed in the next section.

- See the big picture.
- Think before speaking.
- Get the issues out.
- Do what you do best.
- Consider the worst-case scenario.
- Maintain your integrity.
- Ask for your adversary's help.
- Acknowledge and apologize.
- Enjoy the show.
- Trust God's promises.
- Work within the system.
- Respect your adversary.
- Flip flop.
- Walk away.
- Bring in an outside mediator.
- Let the conflict sharpen you.
- Forgive them. Forgive yourself.
- Relish the competition.

You could stop reading, laminate this list, and simply refer to it every time you're looking to dissipate any unwanted conflict. But then you'd miss the stories behind these remarkable strategies!

Every conflict provides tempting responses for us to stir the pot and make it worse—to escalate. But every conflict also has triggers to calm the storm and turn it in your favor—to de-escalate. It's really your choice, but I implore you…don't take the bait to escalate.

CHAPTER 5

CASE STUDIES
IN CONFLICT

For the next twenty-two short vignettes, we're borrowing a tactic found in hundreds of children's picture books, business parables, and self-help books: stories with a moral.

Aesop pioneered the idea. Remember how reading about the tortoise's victory over the hare confirmed that slow and steady wins the race? Aesop's fables also taught us valuable takeaways such as "never cry wolf," "necessity is the mother of invention," and "look before you leap."

Jesus told parables, many of which end with a question. After telling the parable known as "The Good Samaritan," Jesus asked, "Which of these three do you think was a neighbor to the man who fell into the hands of robbers?" (Luke 10:36).

In Matthew, Jesus tells the story of two sons told by their father to go work in the vineyard. One said, "I will not," but later changed his mind and went. The other said, "I will, sir," but did not go. Jesus asked the gathered crowd, "Which of the two did what his father wanted?" (Matthew 21:31).

Just so, you have the responsibility to read these twenty-two tales of real-life conflict with discernment. *What are the takeaways? How would I handle this situation? Which of these life lessons apply to my current conflict?* Like life, you'll see some clashes are more critical or life-changing than others.

As you read, take a few moments to consider if and how the adversaries on both sides applied the Four Factors to their conflict. Did they have clear, heartfelt goals, thoroughly assess the risks, try to see their adversary's point of view, and approach the conflict with optimism?

In many cases you have to read between the lines, but you will see how the resolution was more satisfying (and often a win for both sides) when the Four Factors were taken into consideration.

Along the way, you'll discover resolution strategies that are surprising and creative. Some reflect the kind of practical application that might be taught in a business class. Some are just good old-fashioned common sense. Don't be surprised if you can immediately apply one of these strategies to a current vexing conflict in your life. Some you'll store up for future use.

You can skip around, but I recommend you don't skip any of these vignettes altogether. You may think the one on union negotiations, buying a car, or confronting your teenage daughter regarding her shorts that are too short doesn't apply to you. But there could be principles tucked inside those lessons that apply to your exact conflict.

In no particular order, you'll read about conflicts from history, film, biblical times, business, family life in the twenty-first century, and other situations to which you can relate.

Let's start with a difference of opinion that might make you nod your head and smile, but also delivers one of the great truths when it comes to resolving conflict. This true story from early in my own marriage suggests that a little common sense and open communication go a long way—and sometimes the resolution is right in front of you.

BUY TWO JARS OF PEANUT BUTTER:
Imagine an easy answer to conflict

For the first several years of our marriage, Rita and I took turns suffering through weeks of peanut butter agony. You see, I liked crunchy and she liked creamy. It was a legitimate conflict. But since we loved each other, making a sandwich with peanut butter of the "wrong" consistency was a sacrifice both of us were willing to make. That unselfish sacrifice was the best way—we thought—to de-escalate that turbulent conflict.

Then a miracle happened. At some point, we brought home a jar of crunchy before the jar of creamy was gone. That's when we realized one of the great secrets of conflict resolution: sometimes the answer is ridiculously easy.

What about any of your current conflicts? Might there be an easy answer that you have totally overlooked? Consider all your relationships.

Are you part of one of those families that consistently arrives at church service on edge every Sunday morning? Instead of searching for lost shoes and screaming, "We're late! Let's go!" take a moment to set out clothes the night before and start corralling everyone to leave the house fifteen minutes earlier.

As a consultant or employee, you take voluminous notes at the initial assignment meeting. But conflict ensues because you go back to that project manager for clarification again and again. Instead, at that first meeting, keep asking questions and don't wrap things up until you actually have jotted down the kernel of a solution for the problem. (Don't reveal it until you flesh it out for a later meeting.)

Between two friends, teammates, or coworkers, is a nasty-sounding accusatory text causing conflict? There's a good chance the tone was misinterpreted. Get those two in the same room and have the sender read the text out loud. That exercise alone—or perhaps a brief clarifying discussion—may provide an easy resolution.

Tired of bumping elbows at the dinner table with your left-handed brother? Switch chairs.

Tired of complaints because one sibling got more ice cream? Have one child dish it out and the other get first choice. Or try switching to ice cream bars.

In some cases which involve the letter of the law, the simple revision of a contract clause or policy might make a conflict go away. An apartment lease agreement prohibiting four-legged creatures prevents the kid in 4C from getting a turtle. But the intent of the clause was really directed at dogs and cats, while allowing birds and fish. (Turtles may have four legs, but they would surely be allowed.)

In families, on teams, among neighbors, even in competitive business environments, most people want to live in peace. Too often in the middle of a conflict, we imagine the worst-case scenario. But the answer might be as easy as getting the two parties to talk it out, clarifying a phrase on a contract, extending a little grace or breathing room, finding a quick compromise, or buying a second jar of peanut butter.

Application

You know that vexing problem you are having with your manager, best friend, teenager, personal trainer, editor, pastor, dog groomer, doorman, or roommate? What is it that you really want? Can you imagine coming up with a solution so simple that you simultaneously slap your foreheads and say, "Why didn't we think of this earlier?"

Without getting into specifics, let's consider what that answer might look like:

- Taking turns
- Scheduling a month in advance
- Sending a reminder text
- Using different colored pens
- Getting a third party to do it
- Starting from scratch
- Putting up a fence, partition, or deflector shield
- Finding a better app
- Giving it a different name or title
- Asking a professional for insight
- Buying a second, identical tool
- Attaching a tracking device
- Seeing what the Bible says

If none of these apply—or don't spark a parallel idea—then take a moment to gather a few friends and brainstorm other easy answers.

The point is one we're going to repeat several times in the pages to follow. We too easily assume the worst or get bogged down in the negatives, when really the ability to de-escalate is just an inspiration or an inch away.

When your subconscious whispers, *There must be a better way*, don't ignore it. Instead devote your next long drive or walk in the woods to finding an easy answer to that conflict. Expect an *aha!* moment. As for me, I do my best thinking in the shower.

Strategy

Not to make light of your conflicts and challenges, but is it possible that you're overlooking an easy answer? We've all done that. We get so bogged down in the enormity of the problem that we overlook the simple.

The best example I know is the story of the semi-trailer truck that grinds to a halt wedged under a railroad bridge. Cops, firefighters, engineers, county officials, and transportation experts gather to assess the situation. Watching for several minutes is a boy on a bike who finally whispers something to one of the officers. About a half hour later the truck driver is happily on his way to the nearest filling station to get his eighteen tires filled back up to the proper air pressure.

ESCALATE

By settling for the status quo. By assuming the worst. By thinking that a longtime conflict is just something you have to live with. When that happens, you're escalating by default.

DE-ESCALATE

Go ahead and assess the timewasters, irritations, gridlocks, and stumbling blocks in your life. Decide what matters and expect a solution. Maybe think like a kid. Look at your next conflict as a puzzle, not a problem.

HONOR THE CHAIN OF COMMAND:
Conflict within an organizational chart

Family is family. Friends are friends. At the end of every squabble, the landing spot is reconciliation. That's the worthy goal. Not so in the dog-eat-dog world of business.

Raise your hand if your most grueling conflicts are on the job where everyone is looking out for their own best interests, trying to snag a more impressive title, or hoping to survive the next downsizing.

When it comes to family, friends, and neighbors, you're stuck with each other. Somehow you learn to live with minor conflicts. Eventually the quirk or foible goes away or you decide it's not really a big deal. But that never happens at work. On-the-job irritations endure. Impatience and resentment fester. Money, influence, power, and job security are all on the line. You begin to think that something needs to be done, and you're the one who is going to do it!

In the workplace, we observe how aggression or pretension seems to gain respect. In the process of earning our paycheck, paying our taxes, and providing for our family, we find ourselves in a battle against an opponent who may not officially be "evil," but is definitely working to advance their own selfish agenda.

Your gut instinct and even your God-given intuition tell you the reasonable and virtuous thing to do is stand up for what's right, stand up for yourself, and slay that giant.

How do you know when that is? What's the secret to knowing when to back down and when to fight back? And are business relationships different from personal relationships? My friend Bradley's story might illuminate this perplexing predicament.

For most of his life, Bradley's natural instinct was to respond to conflict as a warrior. Diplomacy was for wimps. In heading up research and development (R&D) for his company he had learned to be diligent in his work, which included fact-finding, determining product limitations, and standing by his well-reasoned decisions. Unfortunately, some of the data Bradley was gathering wasn't exactly what other departments wanted to hear.

Not surprisingly, in many companies, R&D and marketing are often at odds. Marketing wants to make wild claims, but sometimes the folks in research are required by law to pull the plug on a product claim or promise that just isn't true. As a result, the head of marketing in this real-life example regularly communicated to upper management that Bradley was undercutting the work of her creative team. Savvy in office politics, she even went to management insisting that Bradley schedule and process all research through her, effectively placing R&D under the marketing umbrella.

To make matters more difficult, at the time that marketing manager was a rising star in the company. Bradley knew he needed a plan to increase his credibility and perceived value to the company. Talking it out with some veterans in the corporate world, he came up with a seven-point strategy that worked better than he could have imagined.

1. Have a goal in mind. He decided his objective was to gain the respect of upper management, maintain his department's autonomy, and be recognized as the marketing manager's peer.

2. Don't whine. He knew from his years with the company that any complaining would work against him.

3. Don't trash talk. There was a rabid gossip circle in the company, so he kept his harsh thoughts to himself, even being intentional about saying nice things about his adversary.

4. Gain a reputation as a problem solver. One of the functions of Bradley's department was to identify concerns regarding products and services. Any time he brought a problem to his supervisors, Bradley made a point to accompany it with legitimate working solutions.

5. Present a solid case. Bradley knew his research and data were critical to the company's welfare. Before his adversary could belittle the importance of his work, he took a preemptive stance by

equipping key decision makers with easy-to-understand, practical, ethical, and fiscally prudent reasons to trust his data.

6. Include both logic and creativity with every interaction. Bradley was analytical, but he came to realize that many of his colleagues were motivated by emotion.

7. Maintain power. In meetings that included the marketing manager, Bradley needed to exhibit strength, resilience, and assertiveness. He knew he shouldn't follow his instincts and declare all-out war, but he didn't want to be too "nice" and acquiesce to her demands. She was not his friend, and it was okay for management to know that.

This last strategy proved to be instrumental. Bradley presented himself as strong, resourceful, and respectful while the marketing manager did the opposite. She never lost her cool, but her plan had been to stand on her reputation and subtly discredit Bradley's work and commitment to the company. For most healthy organizations, building a cohesive and productive work environment takes priority over rewarding one rising star without a long track record.

Fortunately for Bradley, he was working in a system that valued the diligence and integrity of team players. It's true that if his supervisors had sided with the marketing manager, he may have ended up on the street. But if that happened, he would have been leaving a place where he and his work were not respected. That's the risk you take.

It's worth noting that being a "team player" seems to have the connotation of just going with the flow. But it's more about *going all in*. It's about delivering on a personal promise of reliability, communication, flexibility, and supporting all members of the team. Establishing yourself as a productive and innovative team player may be the surest way to get the boss to take your side in a conflict or potential conflict.

Application

Every conflict is different, which means your own seven-point strategic plan will be different. (And could be longer or shorter.) With the help of wise counselors, you'll want to come up with a comparable list of objectives and strategies to deal with conflicts within your own organization. Bradley's list brought several biblical passages to mind.

> The plans of the diligent lead to profit as surely as haste leads to poverty. (Proverbs 21:5)

> Do not let any unwholesome talk come out of your mouths, but only what is helpful for building others up according to their needs, that it may benefit those who listen. (Ephesians 4:29)

> Have nothing to do with the fruitless deeds of darkness, but rather expose them. (Ephesians 5:11)

> If the godly give in to the wicked, it's like polluting a fountain or muddying a spring. (Proverbs 25:26 NLT)

Corporations, governments, school districts, churches, ministries, and a variety of organizations all have some kind of established hierarchy. While Bradley's story has specific implications for dealing with a work colleague attempting a power grab, the larger application might be for anyone working within a chain of command. Wherever you find yourself in the company pecking order, respect your peers, mentor those ranking below you, and to your superiors present yourself as a valued, resilient, and steadfast member of the team.

Strategy

When engaged in conflict within an established hierarchy, put your effort into defining your role and performing at the highest level. Too many employees try to take on responsibilities outside their job description. Elevate your language. Equip your immediate supervisor with information and solutions. With respect, model an inner strength and stand by your convictions. Gain mentors in and outside of your organization. When victories come, don't gloat.

ESCALATE

By being confrontational and/or whining to management. By kissing up. By gossiping. By seeing problems without solutions.

DE-ESCALATE

Work within the system, honor those in authority, choose words wisely, and champion excellence. Be a true team player. See solutions to problems.

BE READY TO WALK AWAY:
Eliminate car-buying conflicts

A common conflict that many people would love to avoid is negotiating for the best deal on a new car. Some people enjoy the verbal sparring match with the salesperson and find it amusing each time he says, "I'll have to run this past my manager." Others hate it. Just walking into an automobile showroom twists their guts into knots.

Aware of the disdain many people have for the conflict inherent in the car-buying process, some dealerships have begun offering what they call "no haggle pricing." That sounds nice, but I'm skeptical that anyone really drives out with the best possible price. A few years ago I stumbled across a strategy that avoids all negotiation, which means there's no conflict to escalate.

Some background will help. First, I'm not a car guy. If a vehicle starts when I turn the key and meets my capacity requirements—human bodies and/or cargo—then I'm happy. Second, we were trading in Rita's Chrysler Sebring convertible for a more utilitarian vehicle to haul around future grandkids and an occasional piece of furniture or lumber. Third, we had previously owned a variety of minivans from different U.S. manufacturers and knew any version would do the job.

Paging through our local newspaper, a darn good price for a new Dodge Caravan caught my attention. Just over sixteen grand from a dealer five blocks away. The price was tagged with an asterisk leading to an entire block of fine print, but I didn't let that slow me down. I took the newspaper ad into the showroom, and as soon as a salesperson approached me, I pointed to the photo and said, "I'll take it." We sat down, and he wrote up the order which had a final tally of just under twenty-three thousand dollars. Feigning surprise, I again showed him the ad, and he began to explain why that discounted price didn't apply to me. Without any fanfare or fuss, I stood up, thanked him for his time, and gave him my phone number in case he wanted to sell the car for the exact advertised price. By this time, I had not even test-driven the car and had invested less than a half hour at the dealership. It was pretty easy to walk away.

Two days later, the salesperson called me and said they could sell me the car for the price in the newspaper. The deal was done.

Application

There are situations in life that are ripe for conflict and more conflict. We know that going in. Walking into a car dealership is one of them. Other examples include returning a defective appliance, dealing with home repair contractors who find too many things wrong with my home, dealing with auto mechanics who find too many things wrong with my car, that one pain-in-the-neck client, teenagers with smartphones, neighbors with barking dogs, and the landlord who won't fix your rattling A/C. You can probably think of others.

Entering one of these conversations or confrontations, we expect some pushback. (When it doesn't happen, we're surprised and delighted!) With that dread comes some level of preparedness. We might set our jaws anticipating a battle to the death. We script a little speech hoping to calm the water before we wade in. We compose an earnest threat to take our business elsewhere. But in some cases, the best option would be to quietly walk away at the first sign of any squabble.

A mechanic says, "If this were my car, I wouldn't drive it." A barely profitable client makes another round of ridiculous demands without agreeing to further compensation. A roofer won't give you an exact price. A car dealer tries to tack on an extra two grand for dealer prep, destination charges, and documentation fees, or insists on selling you a service contract. You know what to do. Walk away and—if it makes sense—as you separate yourself from the situation put the ball back in their court: "If you can commit to this price or this plan, you know where to reach me." In most cases, there are plenty of other ways to spend a buck or make a buck with much less frustration.

Sure, sometimes you're stuck dealing with a longtime neighbor, non-responsive landlord, or even your own teenager. Still, there are approaches you can take that parallel the idea of "walking away." It might be simply saying some version of, "This situation needs to be addressed, let me know how you're going to rectify the problem." Clarity is key, laying out specific expectations. You don't have to add a threatening "or else…" It's implied. When you walk away, you're actually giving your adversary the power to make things right.

Strategy

In certain situations, if you anticipate a conflict, promise yourself that you'll remove yourself at the first sign of any frustration, resentment, or irritation. (The only alternative is to raise your voice, and that usually just makes things worse.) The walk-away strategy instantly gives you the upper hand. It's especially handy in short-term relationships in which a significant amount of money is the focus of the disagreement. But it also works when you just don't have the time, energy, or patience to deal with an issue in the moment.

ESCALATE

By trying to win an argument you can't win. Or worse, picking a fight with someone who is a professional when you're just an amateur. By yelling. By giving up or giving in.

DE-ESCALATE

If it's not going your way, walk away. Firmly, quietly, with no fuss. Feel free to keep the door open, allowing your adversary to come back when they finally see things your way. Let time work in your favor.

VALUE RELATIONSHIP OVER THE DISPUTE:
When friends are in conflict

The nail bed on my left index finger doesn't produce a smooth fingernail. When I was in high school, I damaged the eponychium on that finger, leaving the nail plate with a malformed cuticle and a permanent distinct groove down the middle of the nail.

It's really not a big deal. But even today, decades later, when that damaged digit does grab my attention, typically I smile and think about my boyhood friend, Chuck, and our youth pastor, Kathy.

As best friends from seventh grade through high school, Chuck and I saw each other through some growing pains and life milestones. Things like first girlfriends, imagining future careers, and spiritual stumbling blocks. One summer, we worked at the same factory. I would be best man at Chuck's wedding.

Chuck was taller and a better athlete, painfully not making the final cut for the varsity basketball team. I wrestled in high school. Which is why we were fairly evenly matched the afternoon we got into a little scuffle walking to his house after school. I'm not sure how it started. He playfully tripped me. I shoved him back. And so on, until it wasn't playful anymore. Chuck got me in a headlock as we rolled down a wooded embankment where my hand got smashed and bloodied against a tree stump. Getting even, I chased him to the park a block from his house and went into full takedown mode. Somehow he jammed his knee. I watched him limp home and assumed our long friendship was over.

The next day Chuck wasn't at school. That afternoon, I slumped down into a chair in Kathy's office at the church and told her my worst fear. *I had lost my best friend.* Wise beyond her years, Kathy said, "Don't you think Chuck values your friendship as much as you do?" My high school brain had not considered that. From the church vending machine I bought a grape Fanta (Chuck's favorite) and walked to his house, following the same route we had navigated tumultuously the day before. Chuck's mom answered the door and instantly knew why I was there. Chuck accepted the Fanta and without any apologies or long speeches we made peace. I don't think we mentioned the scuffle that day or ever again.

Looking back on the life lesson gained so long ago, Kathy was just a few years out of college with a degree in youth ministry. Although it's possible, I doubt her professors covered specifically how to address the crisis of two young men roughhousing their way to almost losing their friendship. But I'm grateful for Kathy's insight and also grateful for the physical reminder I have—on my left index finger—of the value of relationships.

Application

In the course of our lives, there will be a handful of relationships that should be able to survive just about anything. At least, that's a worthy goal. Those cherished relationships—while rare—establish a foundation for enduring all your other relationships. When everyone else is busting your chops or driving you mad, you know there are a handful of people you can trust and count on.

A few strategies regarding how to develop those relationships can be found in the book of 1 Peter.

> Now that you have purified yourselves by obeying the truth so that you have sincere love for each other, love one another deeply, from the heart. (1 Peter 1:22)

> Rid yourselves of all malice and all deceit, hypocrisy, envy, and slander of every kind. (1 Peter 2:1)

> Above all, love each other deeply, because love covers over a multitude of sins. (1 Peter 4:8)

Did you see those three relationship strategies? Living and speaking truth opens your heart to love. Getting rid of malignant thoughts allows relationships to flourish. Love covers the inevitable conflicts that come up in any friendship.

Notice also that these strategies aren't passive. We need to obey truth, rid ourselves of negativity, and love deeply. For sure, sometimes we do need to speak sincere words of brokenness and regret. But often, the relationship itself can be enough. Especially one built on love, trust, and Christian fellowship over a period of time. Do you have a friend or two with whom you can claim that?

That kind of indestructible relationship is also the goal in marriage, but will require an even greater commitment to patience, open doors of communication, honesty, empathy, and all those other habits and traits that would fill a marriage manual.

In the above example from my own youth, it was Kathy's words that opened my eyes to the value of my relationship with Chuck. Her words triggered my course of action, prompting me not to give in to my fears and to make amends with Chuck that very day. If I had not, we have a good idea what would have happened. The rift would have deepened! That's why the Bible also says, "Do not let the sun go down on your anger" (Ephesians 4:26 NASB).

When we think about escalating conflict, responses such as screaming, tattling, pouting, or physical aggression come to mind. But is it possible that ignoring a conflict—letting it fester for weeks or years—is more damaging than all the other ways combined? How many lost friendships, family feuds, and drifting marriages can be traced back to a relatively minor misunderstanding that might have been avoided if one of the injured parties had made a simple gesture of apology? It could be a silent gift or just showing up. Or a few simple words might be all it takes. "I'm really sorry." "I hope you can forgive me." "My bad."

In other words, in a relationship built on love or deep friendship, sometimes less is more. Especially if the matter is dealt with promptly. Still, as true as that may be, this short chapter does not give license for taking any relationship for granted. Be warned. Never forget that hurtful rifts have the potential to destroy a marriage or lifelong friendship. In some cases, restoring trust, respect, and devotion may require not less, but more attention, more listening, and more TLC.

It may be weird for a while. Some broken trusts may have to be reestablished. An authentic apology may be necessary. If possible, allow your Christ-centered relationship to lay down a smooth path for giving and receiving that apology. If the relationship feels different afterward, consider it part of the growing process.

Bottom line. If you find yourself in conflict with a true friend or loved one, once you both realize that your relationship has more value than the conflict, the resolution is within reach.

Strategy

Even in longtime relationships filled with mutual respect and appreciation, conflict happens. Perhaps the answer is easier than you think. Simply come together and recommit.

ESCALATE

By giving up on an important relationship. By not dealing with a conflict ASAP. By assuming time heals all wounds, when actually it can lead to festering and decay—and sometimes permanent disengagement. Yikes.

DE-ESCALATE

In humility and trust, mutually acknowledge that what you have is way bigger and more cherished than the conflict. Trust love.

TRUST THE LARGER PROMISE:
A lesson in conflict management from Abraham

When we first meet Abram (whose name would later be changed to Abraham), he was engaged in an astonishing conversation with God. Abram's father, Terah, had set out to lead the entire extended family from Ur to Canaan, pretty much from the Persian Gulf to the Mediterranean Sea. For some unknown reason, Terah decided not to finish the journey, settling in Haran, where he would die at the ripe old age of 205.

Genesis 12 begins with God making a clear promise to Abram, who had just taken on the task of being the new patriarch of the family.

> The Lord had said to Abram, "Go from your country, your people
> and your father's household to the land I will show you.
> I will make you into a great nation,
> and I will bless you;
> I will make your name great,
> and you will be a blessing.
> I will bless those who bless you,
> and whoever curses you I will curse;
> and all peoples on earth
> will be blessed through you."
> (Genesis 12:1–3)

This was not a dream or gut feeling. This was not an appeal from his wife, Sarai. Abram literally heard the voice of God delivering both instructions and a promise. Essentially, "Do what I say and you will become the most important person on the planet." Biblical scholars are fond of praising Abram's faithfulness, but I'm not that impressed. Stepping out of a tent in the middle of the Egyptian desert and hearing a life-changing promise from a clear heavenly voice would gain anyone's attention and devotion. Nonetheless, Abram deserves credit for his perseverance and role as founder of the Jewish nation.

The passages that follow reveal God slowly but surely keeping His promises. He delivers Abram from a famine, rescues him from Pharaoh, and makes him wealthy in silver, gold, and livestock. God's generosity was so profound that even Abram's self-centered nephew Lot, who had been tagging along, somehow acquired his own massive herds. We later read their livestock were so plentiful the land couldn't support them, which led to quarrels among Lot's and Abram's herdsmen.

How does Abram address the conflict? And what lessons apply today? As head of the family, Abram could have played his elder card and assigned a desolate few acres to Lot or banished him to find his own pastures. Instead, Abram surprised Lot with an offer.

> So Abram said to Lot, "Let's not have any quarreling between you and me, or between your herders and mine, for we are close relatives. Is not the whole land before you? Let's part company. If you go to the left, I'll go to the right; if you go to the right, I'll go to the left."
>
> Lot looked around and saw that the whole plain of the Jordan toward Zoar was well watered, like the garden of the Lord, like the land of Egypt. (This was before the Lord destroyed Sodom and Gomorrah.) So Lot chose for himself the whole plain of the Jordan and set out toward the east. The two men parted company: Abram lived in the land of Canaan, while Lot lived among the cities of the plain and pitched his tents near Sodom. (Genesis 13:8–12)

No doubt, Abram could have claimed the best land. But he already had something better. Much better. Abram had confidence in the promises of God. That freed him to act unselfishly, allowing Lot to choose the well-watered Jordan Valley for his herds. At the time, it's not clear whether Lot knew he was moving his own family and servants into the vicinity of Sodom and its lustful enticements.

But God knew, thereby protecting Abram and his heirs from those temptations.

It turns out Abram's trust was rewarded. After the uncle and nephew went their separate ways, God spoke again to Abram.

> Look around from where you are, to the north and south, to the east and west. All the land that you see I will give to you and your offspring forever. I will make your offspring like the dust of the earth, so that if anyone could count the dust, then your offspring could be counted. Go, walk through the length and breadth of the land, for I am giving it to you. (Genesis 13:14–17)

Abram's trust led to God confirming and even sweetening his covenant. That's something worth remembering.

As we make choices and take charge of our own lives, God has given us common sense and worldly wisdom. Unfortunately, those decision-making tools are not foolproof and can lead us into unsavory situations and major conflicts. Like Abram, we have the ability to enter any conflict with the full awareness that nothing could compare to knowing God and trusting His promises. While Abram heard God's assurances in the desert, we are fortunate to have access to God's promises to all authentic Christians throughout the pages of the Bible. Here are just a few:

> God will meet all your needs according to the riches of his glory in Christ Jesus. (Philippians 4:19)

> Come to me, all you who are weary and burdened, and I will give you rest. (Matthew 11:28)

If you declare with your mouth, "Jesus is Lord," and
believe in your heart that God raised him from the dead,
you will be saved. (Romans 10:9)

Take delight in the Lord, and he will give you the desires
of your heart. (Psalm 37:4)

Those are clear promises of provision, rest, salvation, and your
heart's desire—all reserved for those who trust in the name of the
Lord. If that includes you, then in the middle of a quarrel—or in
anticipation of a potential quarrel—it might be a good idea to pause
and ask yourself, *What's the worst that can happen? I already have
been promised more than I deserve!* That realization might have
been going through Abram's mind when he gave Lot the first choice
of property rights. He was regularly communicating with the Creator of the Universe and had unconditional assurances that his life
would have meaning and merit.

The ability to see the big picture—the larger promise—makes
all the difference in negotiations, disputes, and relationships. If the
goal is to win, you already have.

Application

You may never have walked out of your tent, looked at the
stars, and heard God's clear voice, but you do have His promises—
hundreds of them, all recorded in the Bible, plus a few more personal promises God may have written on your heart.

Armed with that confidence, you have a surprising amount
of freedom. Once in a while, it really is okay to lose an argument,
yield to unfair demands, or come out with the short end of the
stick. You can even let your nephew have first choice of a prime

piece of real estate. Or let your work colleague take credit for a project you did jointly. Or let your spouse have the last word. Because you know that everything is going to be okay. Like Abram, you've got God's word. (Even more so, because you've seen the fulfillment of God's ultimate promise in the life, death, and resurrection of Jesus.)

Of course, you still want to use every tool in your toolbox to make wise decisions and be at peace with the outcomes of any conflicts you face. You also don't want to be a chump, allowing yourself to be bullied or taken advantage of.

Whatever the resolution, recognize you can hang on to a larger promise—or an entire book filled with promises—which allows you to grin and bear it. Because in many ways, you have the last laugh.

Strategy

As we walk through life—in the best of times and the worst of times—we can have confidence in God's plan. Jeremiah 29:11 promises, "'For I know the plans I have for you,' declares the Lord, 'plans to prosper you and not to harm you, plans to give you hope and a future.'" Often, we may not see what lies ahead, but we can count on the bigger promise. Said another way, "We're not home yet." If we agonize or complain about the temporary losses and frustrations of this world, we lose some of the joy in our journey. Don't let that happen.

ESCALATE

By needing to win every earthly battle. By living with a host of regrets. By whining when things don't go *your* way.

DE-ESCALATE

See the big picture. Uncover God's promises. Maybe even go against conventional wisdom and let the other side get the first or best choice. Imagine what that does to your witness for the Gospel.

SYSTEMATIC DIPLOMACY:
High-stakes conflicts in union negotiations

Can you imagine a situation more prone to conflict than contract negotiations between one of the Big Three automakers and the United Auto Workers union (UAW)?

My friend and mentor, Mike, served as a labor relations manager for a midwestern district of General Motors back in the 1970s. His stories from that era often include a hint of dark humor as he recalls the posturing, spin, and absurdity of corporate vs. union politics. Most of his negotiations with the union bargaining committee were respectful and productive, but not always.

Mike specifically remembers many long nights and weekends when the media were led to believe that active, thoughtful dialogue was helping move the next contract closer to being signed. Actually, as Mike put it, the union reps were sitting across the hall with no intention of coming to the table for days or weeks. Everyone on both sides knew nothing productive would happen until the old contract was just about to expire.

One Friday afternoon, Mike decided to send his negotiating team home until Monday because they had already wasted several weekends waiting for the union reps to even enter the room. Mike thought he was doing everyone a favor by allowing both sides to spend time with their families. Flipping on the evening news at home, he was surprised to hear his name mentioned disdainfully in one of the lead stories, describing how the tyrannical and heartless multinational corporation had abruptly suspended negotiations with the blameless union representatives. Mike's corporate bosses knew the media spin had come from the UAW, but they were displeased with him nonetheless.

When both sides finally did come to the table, Mike used an organized, step-by-step agenda to guide the arbitration while minimizing conflict—a blueprint for any high-stakes negotiation. Each step required agreement from both sides before moving to the next.

First, he would create a detailed list of all the issues on all sides. Reflecting back, Mike remembers heated debates regarding smoking on the assembly line, bathroom breaks, access to telephones, whether workers changed in and out of uniforms on their own time or on company time, and other more obvious issues such as wages, vacations, and pensions.

Second, he would literally divide the issues into three piles. The first stack he called "good news" because it contained issues that could be immediately resolved. Often, that first pile included duplicate demands. Eliminating redundancies shortened the list and created an atmosphere that progress was being made. Also, sometimes semantics in a contract created divisiveness. Simply choosing less inflammatory words could resolve some of the union demands.

The other two piles were a bit more difficult. One stack was issues Mike hoped to resolve in friendly dialogue while the final pile included issues that would likely require a visit from the big guns from Detroit. A crucial caveat from Mike's bosses was to avoid making any unsanctioned concessions to a union demand at one small factory in the Midwest because within days every worker in the country would expect the same benefit, salary increase, or special treatment.

The third step Mike administered was having each side rank all issues in order of importance. When dealing with multiple issues, that revealing activity helped both sides see the bigger picture and begin to visualize a pathway to a final accord.

Eventually, in most cases, a federal mediator would come in to hammer out the final sticking points. The impartial mediator was more than just a numbers guy. He or she was also an expert on human behavior, stimulating productive dialogue, mitigating passive-aggressive behavior and other counterproductive conduct, and preventing stalemates. In many cases, outside mediators would have both sides complete a confidential questionnaire which would help them know when the terms were getting closer to compromise or partial resolution.

One of the perhaps unspoken secrets to successful negotiations is that neither side concedes too much too soon. Way before coming to the table, representatives would privately determine numbers and stipulations they could "live with." If one side revealed those terms too soon, the other side would gain "the upper hand," leaving the negotiations to grind to a halt because there remained no bargaining room as talks progressed.

The process would typically take a few days, but could stretch out for weeks.

At the final contract signing, if negotiators came out of that smoke-filled room at the eleventh hour worn down and worn out, union workers and corporate stockholders would feel like they had been represented well. Mike recalls that somehow both sides would declare themselves hard-fought winners to their constituents, while spinning to the public how they had made huge sacrifices.

The bigger point is that a system was in place to minimize escalation. Both sides knew if they kept their cool, the assembly lines would keep rolling and the workers would keep getting paid. Of course, at the end of negotiations sometimes the prices of cars had to go up. But such is the nature of capitalism.

For negotiations on that scale to unfold year after year, a proven system had to be in place. Professionals had to be brought in. Personalities had to remain in check. Compromises had to be made. Gamesmanship, bluffing, and grandstanding were all expected parts of the negotiations. But so also were mutual respect and even an unspoken sense of empathy for the other side. Most importantly, both sides had to—eventually—show up in good faith and realize what was at stake.

Mike told me he did negotiate through some production stoppages and picketing, but mostly he was part of a formal system that worked. For both sides.

Application

Most of life's conflicts are between two regular folks and official rules are nowhere to be found. But at the executive offices of Fortune 500 companies and the headquarters of powerful labor unions, especially in previous decades, negotiators turned often to fat binders full of regulations, procedures, and strategies to help guide contract negotiations.

Today, the shifting economy has reduced the ranks of organized labor, the rooms aren't smoke-filled, and much of the mediation takes place remotely. But collective-bargaining showdowns still employ rules and strategies that bring accord, not division. In your next conflict or negotiation, you would do well to take advantage of those proven principles, especially if you have time to think through what you really want to achieve.

There are questions to answer and actions to take. Here's where the Four Factors will come in handy.

What do you really want? Write down your key issues. Prioritize them. Make note of which issues might be immediately resolved, especially looking at areas of miscommunication or misinterpretation. Be honest with yourself and imagine your adversary's point of view to determine which issues might be the trickiest sticking points. Will those issues ever be resolved? Is there a deadline? Should you invite someone, like Mike, to represent your best interest? Should you invite an impartial third party to mediate? Who would that be? If specific numbers are involved—or an issue that has degrees or alternatives—have you set minimum acceptable terms? Do you know what your starting offer will be? (Remember, don't give away too much too soon.) What are the ramifications if you or your adversary walks away from the table? Are you capable of bluffing and hardball negotiating?

Some people love the gamesmanship. Others, not so much. If the goal is to come to an agreement, the idea of compromise needs to be on the table. A "strike" may happen, but eventually both sides need to resume talks. As indicated in other chapters, compromise is not necessarily the goal in all conflicts. But high-stakes negotiations are typically resolved by minimizing escalation and looking for that win-win.

Strategy

If you're actually in a high-stakes negotiation that threatens the well-being of hundreds of families and the future of a valuable organization, please access resources and experts beyond this book.

On the other hand, the above lessons of systematic diplomacy would serve you well any time you find yourself in legitimate real-life negotiations. Whether that's negotiating your own salary, a contract with an architect, the timeline on a construction project, the purchase price of a used lawnmower, which plot you're going to claim and tend in a community garden, or what networks and channels you want from your cable provider. Simply put, the goal is to stay at the table until you find that sweet spot delivering a win for both sides.

ESCALATE

By dominating, abandoning, or never even showing up to the conversation. By lying, manipulating the media, or not playing by the rules.

DE-ESCALATE

Get the issues out and accept the fact that both sides will have to make sacrifices. Look for small steps early. Expect some bumps. Suggest bringing in outside help. Know your acceptable parameters before beginning the negotiation. Assume that both sides— eventually—want to come to amicable terms.

HIT BOTTOM TOGETHER:
Marriage conflicts can lead to marriage milestones

This particular strategy for conflict resolution is reserved for married couples. (Or perhaps very close friends.) It's based on the idea that virtually every couple will arrive at a point in their marriage when the two of you realize things can no longer go the way they're going. You have hit bottom.

That crossroads could come in the form of a dramatic altercation that shakes the windows, frightens the neighbors, and makes headlines. More likely it will be a quiet, crushing moment in the course of everyday life. Depending on how that husband and wife respond, such a moment can make or break their marriage.

A story might help you understand this principle.

Once upon a time a boy named Jay was full of optimism and potential. Plus he was kinda cute, so Rita said yes when Jay got on one knee and presented her with a not-so-huge one-quarter-carat diamond ring. The fact that he had not achieved much didn't matter because his new wife had a lot of faith in her young husband.

Until she didn't.

You see, before long Jay and Rita had two small boys and were a couple months behind on their mortgage. Silly Jay was trying to earn a living selling law books to corporate attorneys, and he was not very good at it. He slogged around the Chicago Loop carrying a twenty-six-pound briefcase filled with samples. His three poly-ester three-piece suits were getting shabbier and shabbier. His lone pair of black wingtips that once belonged to his grandfather had holes in their soles. Every month, he got further and further behind on his sales quotas.

Still, even in the midst of the job angst, their life was not all bad. Their two boys were healthy and smart. They were plugged in to a good church and even had friends praying for them. Every evening, Rita kissed her husband and asked about his day. That was a good thing. And sometimes a hard thing.

Here, it's worth pointing out that guys often have their identity and self-esteem wrapped up in the success they experience on the job. Maybe it shouldn't be that way, but it is.

Not surprisingly, Jay's optimism was disappearing. His formerly abundant potential seemed nowhere to be found. The world

Jay had once hoped to conquer was beating him up and dragging him down. But Rita still loved him. Which is why she did what she did.

She could have screamed at Jay to work harder. She could have pretended everything was okay. She could have taken the two boys and moved home to her parents' house. She could have complained to all her friends and made his life miserable until he moved out.

Instead, she spoke. Rita did not raise her voice. She did not accuse. As she sat on the floor of their tiny living room, she looked at her husband standing in the kitchen doorway and quietly said, "I don't have faith in you anymore."

It hurt Jay to hear that. But somehow, those were the exact right words at the exact right time. Even though they had been married less than five years, Rita knew her husband well enough that she could speak into his life like no one else. She was telling Jay that he was not alone. They were partners, and any crisis needed to be faced with honesty, commitment, and communication. As he stood in the doorway, Jay experienced the worst and best moment of his life.

No, he didn't become a better salesman. That would have been impossible. But Jay did write those seven words on a 3x5 card and pushpin it on the wall above his desk: "I don't have faith in you anymore." Jay stopped feeling sorry for himself. He hustled a little more. He reevaluated his gifts, passions, and career options. Jay and Rita intentionally spent more time talking about goals, hopes, dreams, and God's plan for their lives.

That summer, Jay changed careers. His first job as an entry-level copywriter at a small advertising agency on Michigan Avenue in Chicago was a direct result of those husband-and-wife talks about all the things that really matter. When Jay told Rita the new job would actually reduce their income, she didn't hesitate. The young mother proved once again that she knew her husband and exactly what he needed to hear. Rita said, "We'll make it work."

Thirty years later, Jay still can't sell anything. But the bills are getting paid, their four sons and daughter are all healthy, productive members of society, four daughters-in-law have joined the family, and so have eight perfect grandchildren. They all get along. No one has missed a meal. And Rita and Jay have one more little joke that gets sprinkled into their current conversations about goals, hopes, dreams, and God's plan for their lives. Thinking back to that 3x5 card, Jay will say, "Do you have faith in me?" And Rita will get a twinkle in her eye and say, "For now."

That's one of my favorite stories, first shared in my book *52 Ways to Connect as a Couple* as well as at numerous marriage retreats. At those conferences, I'll ask for a show of hands from any couples who have "hit bottom." Almost half of the married couples raise their hands. When I follow up with the question, "Isn't it awesome?" those couples nod their heads and sometimes even break into a round of light applause. Like Rita and me, they look back at that moment of truth in marriage with gratitude. They recognize that working through that desperate life challenge brought them closer and typically prompted a much-needed course correction in their marriage.

Of course, the plunge into that abyss is different for every marriage. Some go way darker or way deeper when they hit bottom. That includes financial collapse, infidelity, spiritual battles, uncontrolled anger, deceit, broken trust, and conflicting priorities. But looking back to recall the severity of the adversity you survived makes the restoration and fresh commitment ever so much sweeter.

Application

Even the best marriages will endure an occasional disagreement. Perhaps even entire seasons of disagreement that go on for an uncomfortably long time. The principle of *hitting bottom together* is all about prioritizing relationship over the problem. Realizing that, indeed, two heads are better than one...allowing two hearts to come together. Remember how the two of you promised to leave and cleave as described in Paul's letter to the Ephesians, quoting Genesis? *"For this reason a man will leave his father and mother and be united to his wife, and the two will become one flesh"* (Ephesians 5:31). With those vows, you were committing to work toward "being on the same page." To study, know, and accept each other's strengths and weaknesses. You were promising to invest your heads and hearts into solving any crisis, large or small. From minor potholes in the road of life to bottomless pits of despair.

If one of you is hurting, remember your spouse was given to you (and vice versa) as a helpmate, partner, advisor, encourager, and sounding board. And because you have become one flesh, your beloved is hurting too!

When you stand shoulder-to-shoulder together, looking up at how far you have to climb, it becomes readily apparent that you can't get out alone. If one of you stands at the top of the pit mocking, blaming, or denying any responsibility, then your wedding vows were a deceit, merely for show. But if you hit bottom together, you will both be there with no choice but to reach toward, lift up, boost, and support each other as you crawl out into the sun.

By the way, there's a very good chance that it's God who allowed you to fall. But don't be angry with Him, because He is also the One who pulls you out to set your feet on solid rock.

Don't worry about if and when you hit bottom. Because it's so common, you'll actually want to prepare for it. Expect it. Probably not in the first year of marriage. And probably not after you've been married a few decades. But somewhere in between. You'll both see it coming, but it might be a courageous word from one of you that leads to those critical heartfelt discussions marked by respect, openness, and commitment.

I don't recommend either of you do something foolish or mean-spirited with the goal of forcing those frank conversations. You may be choosing a moment in which your spouse doesn't have the desire or ability to join you in a self-inflicted abyss.

Also, I can't emphasize enough that Rita carefully considered her words. She said the right thing at the right time. You'll want to make sure you do the same for your partner.

Here's another warning: this idea of speaking truth into the life of your spouse does not give either spouse permission to nitpick minor issues that are really just part of the human experience.

Finally, while hitting bottom together and climbing out together is a beautiful and beneficial experience, I cannot recommend doing it more than a few times in any relationship.

Strategy

Honor your marriage always. Serve each other. Fill each other's love cups. Speak each other's love language. Know what brings motivation or discouragement to your partner. Make memories and share secrets along the way. Pray together. Trust the promises of 1 Corinthians 13:6–7: "Love does not delight in evil but rejoices with the truth. It always protects, always trusts, always hopes, always perseveres."

Strengthen your marriage now, so that if and when you do hit bottom, you have a combined power to climb out together. Expect that after uniting forces to slay the dragon, you'll be more in love and more committed to your marriage.

ESCALATE
By pretending your marriage will always be carefree and indestructible. Or by brushing aside any lingering regret, difference in priorities, or divisive issue. By neglecting to "cleave." By using words that are destructive without leaving the door open for reconciliation.

DE-ESCALATE
While nurturing your relationship and seeing the big picture, do your best to address concerns as they arise so they don't grow into bigger problems. But when you do truly hit bottom, have the courage to say what needs to be said. Gently. Lovingly. Hopefully. And expect a resolution to that conflict that ultimately strengthens your bond.

SIDESTEP QUIBBLES:
How to avoid most minor relational conflicts
The previous scenario revealed how facing a conflict together can be a turning point which brings couples—or longtime friends—even closer. That positive result of conflict is only possible when couples place a high priority on knowing each other's passions, fears, quirks, and motivations. In other words, what makes your partner tick.

That intimate knowledge will also help prevent the negative outcomes that result from the little digs, insinuations, and thoughtless remarks that can fly so freely in a marriage. You know what I'm talking about. But a few examples from my life—words I've spoken to my own wife—might help:

"I see they opened a new women's fitness center down the street."

"How much was that haircut again?"

"Your way works fine, but my mom used to do it this way."

"Actually, I'm not really hungry. I had a late lunch with Amber from marketing."

"You know, these mugs you bought don't fit in the dishwasher."

To be clear, when I said these things I did not mean what Rita heard. She heard, "You're fat," "You're ugly," "You're a failure," "You're unimportant," and "You're stupid."

Yikes! I would never say such things. But that's the point. Like so many married individuals, most of us don't stop—even for a moment—to consider how our words are received. Husbands, wives, and BFFs could prevent so many minor agitations simply by engaging our brain before putting our mouth in gear.

Even parents—especially parents—should do their best to sidestep quibbles. You have so many important truths and values to pass on to the next generation, why would you risk ticking them off and having them shut down by being hurtful or manipulative? If you're a parent of older kids, you know your words can hugely impact their hearts and minds. After a brief conversation, you've seen them leave the room with head held high, motivated to take their efforts to the next level, or hanging their head because something you said was taken the wrong way.

It's surprising how often words meant to motivate or deliver a simple reminder can be a double-edged sword that wounds the psyche and divides families. Consider the subtext of these innocent words from well-meaning parents.

"Are you getting enough exercise?"

"Why don't you eat an apple instead?"

"Are you sure you can do that?"

"I see the O'Grady kid broke into the starting lineup."

"You missed several spots when you mowed the lawn."

"Well, maybe you could run lights or be on the tech crew."

"Did you know there are 140 calories in a can of Coke?"

"You got your 'A' in math again, but you need to put that same effort into English and Social Studies."

Now it's possible your child will take your words as motivation. But I hope you see how these statements are not really advice, wisdom, or encouragement. They're pretty much calling your child fat, incompetent, or a disappointment to you.

Here's the question to ask yourself: *Did you know what you were really saying before you said it?*

In some cases, it's not what you say, but when. In a longer conversation, questions can be asked, advice can be shared thoughtfully, and stories can be told that put your words in context. Words said in passing often do the most damage.

Whether it's your child, spouse, parent, close friend, or long-time work colleague, let's all pledge to do a little more thinking before we speak. Why are we less thoughtful with our words to the most important people in our lives? We deliver one-line zingers to loved ones that we would never say to a salesclerk or casual work colleague.

If we're serious about de-escalating the conflict in our lives, speaking patterns with family and friends might be the best place to start.

Application

There probably is not incendiary subtext in everything you say. But your opinions and pronouncements carry more weight than you think. I know backstabbing, slander, and smear tactics are not your style. Unfortunately, today's culture has a way of leading people to think the worst.

When you ask, "What's for dinner?" your spouse may go on the defensive, exasperated that tonight's menu is being prejudged when really you just wanted to know what smelled so good.

When you walk into the conference room and ask, "Anyone seen Shoemaker?" your workmates may think you're throwing him under the bus for being late, when really you just want to warn him his car is about to be towed.

People are always looking for subtext. They expect it. When texting or video chatting, it's even more difficult to determine the emotions or motivations of communications. Which means quibbling—or making a mountain out of a molehill—is only going to increase.

So how can we stop this two-way miscommunication—the barrage of thoughtless comments and the equally toxic cynicism of thinking the worst about things people say?

It's a three-part plan. One, think about how your words will be received before you speak. Two, take the time and add enough information to your statement so the listener really knows what you're trying to say. Three, in our conversations, let's be a little more optimistic about the intentions of people we know and love. Not everyone has a hidden or sinister agenda.

If the goal is to de-escalate our daily conversations, let's begin with including more compassion, encouragement, and hope in our attitudes. And if that's difficult for you, then maybe consider this piece of solid advice: "Whoever derides their neighbor has no sense, but the one who has understanding holds their tongue" (Proverbs 11:12).

Strategy

Pausing before speaking is the main takeaway of this chapter. But really, in so many cases, we plow ahead with our words even though we know they will be hurtful to the hearer. So sometimes we need to just bite our tongue. Or maybe say something overtly uplifting instead. Grandma's advice still rings true: "If you can't say something nice, don't say anything at all."

ESCALATE

By being clever and witty at others' expense. By making passive-aggressive statements that push loved ones away.

DE-ESCALATE

Think before speaking. When someone speaks words that feel hurtful, don't assume the worst. Don't let quibbles spoil your most important—or any—relationships. Or here's an idea: try being nice.

ACCEPT THE POSSIBILITY OF THE WORST-CASE SCENARIO:
How confidence overcomes conflict

While selling industrial spray nozzles for chemicals and cleaning agents, my friend Bernie developed a can't-lose strategy for dealing with pesky client conflicts.

If an engineer or plant manager was raising a stink about the effectiveness or reliability of one of Bernie's products, he would commit to doing everything possible to troubleshoot the problem. But occasionally the client would cross a line by either asking for the impossible, or for a solution that would require so much effort that it became a money-losing proposition. When facing that kind of lost cause, Bernie's years of experience enabled him to conclude, *We've already lost this business, so whatever happens happens.*

In some situations, that attitude brings freedom and may even lead to a fresh perspective and solution to the crisis.

A case in point: when an engineer for a Wisconsin brewery complained repeatedly about the quality of a certain model of spray nozzle, Bernie didn't panic or take it personally. But he did want to get to the root of the problem, so he made a deal with the brewmaster: he would send out one of his engineers, and if the issue couldn't be resolved, there would be no charge. But if the engineer *did* solve the problem, that brewmaster would commit to buying nozzles only from Bernie's company for all ten fermenting tanks as long as they were in the brewing business.

After a couple days of tinkering, the truth came out. It turns out the engineer on staff with the brewery had been modifying the nozzles in an attempt to come up with a design he could patent himself—essentially sabotaging the work of Bernie's company. What's more, the unscrupulous engineer had been insisting on trying different custom configurations of nozzles for almost a year. In the end, the optimal nozzle for the job was right off the shelf, not custom at all. The in-house engineer was fired. The brewmaster was happy. And Bernie gained a customer for life.

In a business context, you typically have to consider the economics when dealing with a frustrating client. You can't just cut them loose at the first sign of any difficulty. Soon enough, you won't have any clients left! But many conflicts come with a point of no return. It's more than you can handle, or it's costing you too much time and effort. As they say, the juice is not worth the squeeze. When you reach that point, it's healthy to imagine life *without* that relationship. Estimate the lost income, but also consider the value of ridding yourself of those frustrations and your own improved workflow. If you forecast a situation better than your current one, then you have your answer and it may be time to cut your losses.

Armed with that confidence, see if you can come up with a final proposal. Perhaps with the help of trusted advisors, before abandoning the relationship, you may want to consider one more option that could lead to a win-win. Your final proposal—which may include some kind of dare or challenge—may open the door to new ideas and unexpected answers.

Application

I can't recommend ultimatums as the best way to respond to conflicts. But that's not what Bernie was doing. He wasn't saying, "Do it my way or else!" He was confident in his product and his engineer. He chose intentionally not to lose his cool, risk his reputation, or cheat the brewmaster. Sure, he wanted to save the brewery as a client, but more important was entering the negotiation with the conviction that even the worst-case scenario was not going to mean the end of the world. Money might be lost. But he wouldn't be chasing an impossible scenario and his integrity would be intact. Besides, God was still in control and the sun was still going to come up the next day.

The Bible provides a similar perspective, helping us realize that with God on our side we can get through just about anything. "So we can confidently say, 'The Lord is my helper; I will not fear; what can man do to me?'" (Hebrews 13:6 ESV). In other words, if you're in deep weeds with God you need to make some changes, but if your squabble is with another human there's a good chance you'll be okay.

When you find yourself enduring long-term frustration with a problem client, colleague, neighbor, cousin, business acquaintance, or anyone who has become a thorn in your side, consider taking a step back and asking, "What's the worst that can happen?" It might be something unacceptable, like getting fired or some other hill you aren't prepared to die on. But if the worst-case scenario is something you can live with, then see if you can formulate a solution that might rescue the entire relationship. Start with the goal of solving the crisis and putting this problem behind you. Then—after surrendering the outcome to God—see if you can give the other party a choice. How might they want to solve the problem?

Move ahead with humility, faith, and trust. You may end up losing a little time or money. But the problem will soon be behind you, and you'll be able to sleep at night.

Plus, like Bernie and his problem-solving engineer, you may heroically untangle a knotty situation proving you were right all along.

Strategy

Instead of beating yourself up for not finding an immediate resolution to a conflict, celebrate the fact that—no matter what—you are confident that you can weather the storm. You're not giving up, you're accepting the fact that crud happens. Then, avoid the temptation to build walls or throw stones. Instead of seeing the other party as an adversary, invite them into a partnership while activating both of your best problem-solving abilities.

ESCALATE

By making the same mistakes over and over, depleting your time, energy, and patience. And probably risking other relationships in the process.

DE-ESCALATE

Do what you do best. If it doesn't work, consider the worst-case scenario. Then—partnering with all involved parties—give yourself one last shot and a deadline for finding a resolution. Always maintain your optimism and integrity.

BE A CALM, HEROIC MENTOR:
Cover conflicts with empathy and grace

Let's say you're in conflict with someone who is significantly younger, inexperienced, or new to their position, and you know for certain they're wrong and you're right. One option would be to use your experience and influence to squash them like a bug. Sometimes that just feels great, right? Especially if they haven't shown you the respect you deserve. But let's consider a less-nasty option.

What if you saw this conflict as an opportunity to give that individual a gift? They may not be your favorite person right now, but perhaps you can rise above your feelings and do something heroic.

Start by doing an honest self-assessment of the challenge. Look at the dispute from all sides, making sure you've got your facts and figures right. If there's time, let the situation play itself out, making sure to keep your frustration level close to zero. Then consider how you might turn that conflict into a teachable moment. Think of it as giving grace.

My friend Gary puts together financing packages for midsized companies, often serving as a liaison between borrowers and lending institutions. He successfully cuts deals for his clients because he knows the market and has learned to keep meticulous records. . A landscaping business needed $200,000 and Gary negotiated a reasonably low interest rate which he presented to his client. Unfortunately for the young loan officer, he quoted a rate that was several percentage points off. As a representative of the bank, his misquote would have to be honored and would cut into the bank's profit on the deal. In a mild panic, the loan officer spent a lot of energy casting blame—on everyone but himself.

Gary saw immediately what was going on, knew the quoted rate would stand, and also knew he could straighten out the discrepancy—if necessary—by going to the loan officer's manager. But Gary didn't want to throw the guy under the bus, so he gave the loan officer a chance to make things right on his own. That didn't happen. Gary watched as the younger man seemed to go through many of the stages of grief including denial, anger, blame, bargaining, and finally acceptance.

Looking back, Gary realized the loan officer may have been impaired by inexperience or youthful pride, or maybe he was already in hot water with his superiors for previous mistakes. Gary wanted to keep it professional and—without talking down to him—helped walk the young loan officer through the right channels to concede the error and not lose face.

In a negotiation that has gone off the deep end, it's easy to lose your cool and start pointing fingers. That's when maturity and experience need to rise above the impasse. Aggressively building your case and making sure your voice is heard may not be the best approach. If you can assume a position of quiet strength, you may be able to prevent the relationship from getting adversarial. In an unexpected turn of events, you may find yourself in a temporary mentoring role, helping out a less-experienced colleague or business acquaintance. Years from now, they may have a chance to return the favor.

Still, be on guard when dealing with someone who may be totally wrong but spouts a steady stream of denial and accusations. People in authority may give in to their irritating contentions. They're not making any friends, but often it is the squeaky wheel that gets the grease. There are times to step in and make your own claims loud and clear. But more often than you might think, projecting quiet strength and exhibiting patience is a better choice.

Application

This situation confirms that there is no one set of principles that applies to all conflicts. Resolving most differences, you want the involved parties to honestly express their objectives, allowing everyone to begin judicious negotiating. Here the sticking point was a single number, and only one side could be right. Gary knew that. There really was nothing to debate. No compromises to consider. No logical arguments to present. The young loan officer simply needed a little help to find a way to accept and deal with his error.

At the end of the day, it's possible the younger man still saw Gary as the enemy. But Gary could live with that, knowing his patience and experience benefited all involved and maybe left a lasting lesson.

The idea of turning a conflict into a coaching or mentoring opportunity should be appealing. Most of us go through our day with the single-minded goal of taking care of ourselves (and our loved ones). If you've been blessed with experience in your chosen field, there will come a time when you can use that wisdom to serve others. That's a worthy goal and may even help build the Kingdom of God here on Earth.

Not surprisingly, the Bible encourages the idea of mentoring, emphasizing that with age and maturity comes dignity, wisdom, and self-control. Those are all honorable character traits worth passing on.

> Teach what accords with sound doctrine. Older men are to be sober-minded, dignified, self-controlled, sound in faith, in love, and in steadfastness.
>
> Older women likewise are to be reverent in behavior, not slanderers or slaves to much wine. They are to teach what is good, and so train the young women to love their husbands and children, to be self-controlled, pure, working at home, kind, and submissive to their own husbands, that the word of God may not be reviled.
>
> Likewise, urge the younger men to be self-controlled. Show yourself in all respects to be a model of good works, and in your teaching show integrity, dignity, and sound speech that cannot be condemned, so that an opponent may be put to shame, having nothing evil to say about us. (Titus 2:1–8 ESV)

Make note that the last two verses ("Show yourself...") are talking to all Bible readers of any age and experience, confirming that your good works can provide an important life lesson to your adversary. At the resolution of any conflict, because you stood by your moral principles, your opponent will have "nothing evil to say" about you and will feel a bit of shame for thinking otherwise.

Strategy

Try to see conflict as an opportunity. Not just to negotiate ruthlessly, win an argument, or gain more than you deserve. Often that's the easy part. When conflict comes your way it may be accompanied by a wonderful chance to extend peace, share wisdom, release forgiveness, and/or model dignity to all those involved. In your next negotiation, your greatest victory may be the moment you give grace to someone in desperate need of seeing faith and love in action.

By the way, this is just one example of the many opportunities we have in life to do something honorable for another human as a mentor, colleague, or friend. Do it in secret—without blowing your own horn—and it's a billion times more valuable and more appreciated by that individual you helped out.

Live in the light of Philippians 2:3, "Do nothing out of selfish ambition or vain conceit. Rather, in humility value others above yourselves."

ESCALATE

By winning at all costs and not considering the needs of your adversary. Also by piling on when your opponent is already down.

DE-ESCALATE

Know the truest motivations of your adversary. Engage that empathy we've been talking about. Especially if "victory" is within reach, take time to respect and even mentor the other party. Display humility and grace.

SAY, "I NEED YOUR HELP":
Don't assume conflict

It happens all the time. We're about to enter a situation and we assume the worst. We get defensive before we need to be. In our mind, we presuppose the ticket agent can't find another flight. We anticipate the customer service rep at the 800 number giving us a hard time. We imagine the broker denying our request for a lower interest rate. We assume the auto repair shop is trying to rip us off.

Before we approach that possible adversary, our stomachs churn, our pulses elevate, our minds race, and we arm ourselves for conflict.

In preparation, we write down or make mental notes of all the reasons we're angry, which makes us angrier. But that's good because we think that if we display a little anger our adversary is more likely to back down. After all, "the squeaky wheel gets the grease."

Can you relate? Do you regularly walk into meetings, approach your neighbor, confront your teenager, or point your finger at an innocent counterperson, armed with accusations?

Try this scenario: Instead of thinking the worst, assume the best. Give your adversary—who has not yet displayed any adversarial attributes—every chance to be your hero. Really.

Yes, it's certainly possible that neighbor, car mechanic, ticket agent, or loved one is having a bad day and is also itching for a fight. But it's equally possible they have the desire and ability to meet your exact needs. Wouldn't you want to know that?

To give yourself the best chance of succeeding in your quest, simply begin your verbal exchange with four very powerful words: "I need your help."

You may be surprised to hear that most people don't want to fight you. They don't need more stress in their day. If they have the power to help, often they will. If they can't help, then at least you'll get an honest answer and have the information you need to move forward intelligently.

Most ticket agents want you to get home safely. Most car mechanics want satisfied customers who return with confidence and give good Yelp reviews. Even teenagers want peace in the family.

That person manning the counter who is making minimum wage is trained to do everything she can to make you happy within certain parameters. You don't want her to get fired for doing something against store policy, do you?

So next time you start to anticipate an altercation, instead try those four magic words. Save yourself that stomach acid and teeth grinding. Display patience and understanding. Avoid looking foolish. As Proverbs 14:29 says, "Whoever is patient has great understanding, but one who is quick-tempered displays folly."

It's true that sometimes raising your voice is the fastest way to get someone's attention. Screaming may even move your crisis to the top of their to-do list. But that's no way to live. That's no way to treat those strangers, colleagues, or family members who—like you—are made in God's image. Anger is exhausting.

Smile. Get their attention. Pause. Say, "I need your help." Then explain the situation in a gentle tone with just a hint of desperation. Include other partnering phrases like, "Anything you can do would be great" and "Sorry if this is a hassle."

If necessary, you can highlight your determination with phrases like, "I'm really hoping we can take care of this right here," "This is not how I wanted to spend my day," or "If you don't have the authority to fix this, can you find someone who does?" Done with respect, it may help to add a little passive-aggressive emphasis. Raising your tone is probably more effective than raising your voice.

As you enter into a possible conflict, it's not a bad idea to rehearse a few well-chosen remarks that show you mean business. Still, practically speaking, the most efficient way to solve your problem is to see that person as a partner, not an enemy.

Application

This book is mostly concerned with situations in which others introduce conflict into your life. A bad dude dumps on you. A trusted friend breaks that trust. A business acquaintance doesn't play fair. But sometimes it's the other way around. You're the bad dude. You're the dumper, trust breaker, or unfair business acquaintance.

Please don't pick a fight when there's no reason to do battle. Especially with service people who deal with hassles their entire shift, maybe think of yourself as a bright light in their day. You're giving them a chance to be a hero! In most cases, they really do want to help.

Be winsome in your request. Be firm and expect a fair outcome. Also expect that you might have to practice some patience. You may have to wait your turn or be put on hold. You may even have to listen to their story or, worse, twenty minutes of elevator music. You may not get exactly what you want, but it will probably be the best they can offer. Especially if you start your conversation with a smile and the words, "I need your help."

Strategy

As the saying goes, "You catch more flies with honey." Not sure who said that or why they we "were trapping"re trapping flies, but you get the idea. If you have a strong personality, it might be difficult for you to give the power to your adversary. You may think your self-assured words and unyielding tone will seal your victory. But often they already have the power, not you. The best way to get your way is to let them do their job.

In your quest to get less conflict in your life, it makes sense for you to come to many of your potential flashpoints with a fire extinguisher, not a can of gasoline.

ESCALATE

By thinking your adversary is out to get you. By picking a fight when there's nothing to fight over. By making unreasonable demands of service personnel who have already done everything they can. By assuming that every request you make is going to lead to conflict.

DE-ESCALATE

Say, "I need your help."

ADMIT WHEN YOU'RE WRONG:
When conflict comes full circle

Any thinking politician who serves in some elected capacity for several terms will probably eventually flip-flop on an issue. In many cases, it's a good thing. Early in their political career, they may have had limited information or experience. Later, they become enlightened or endure some life-changing event and suddenly their eyes are opened to a new way of thinking.

Their opponents may call it "waffling" or suggest they made an "illegal U-turn," when the more likely explanation is that they finally saw the light.

Going back several decades, Ronald Reagan was the pro-abortion governor of California. As a presidential candidate and serving in the White House, he would become proudly pro-life.

Going further back, historians note that while he was campaigning, Abraham Lincoln promised to let individual states choose their position on slavery, further stating in his inaugural address that using federal troops within the states would be "among the gravest of crimes." Months later, when the South seceded, he would be forced to use the army in the Civil War. He also signed the Emancipation Proclamation. Did Lincoln flip-flop or, more accurately, was he responding to the circumstances?

Making a U-turn can also be a smart business move. Amazon.com founder Jeff Bezos is best known for changing direction and abandoning highly touted projects. The most notorious example is Amazon Auctions, launched with great fanfare in 1999 to compete with eBay. When the site stalled Bezos efficiently pulled the plug, cutting his losses and turning his attention to more profitable ventures—which, by the way, made him the richest man in the world.

So how about you? In your latest conflict, should you consider some version of a waffling, flip-flopping U-turn? Maybe your adversary is 100 percent correct. Or maybe their way of thinking is 51 percent right. Maybe circumstances have changed since your initial fact finding. Being decisive is good. Being stubbornly boneheaded is not.

Do you have the strength of character to allow for a re-examination or inquest of your current beliefs? Or are your firm convictions worth fighting for? If you're basing your stance on deep spiritual principles in line with biblical truth and backed up by wise counselors, then I apologize for even making the suggestion.

Still, we need to admit that making right decisions on Earth is a constant struggle. In our broken human condition, we are tempted on all sides. We get imperfect information. We go with our guts, turning our backs on research or experience. In the century before Christ, the philosopher Cicero said, "The wise are instructed by reason, average minds by experience, the stupid by necessity and the brute by instinct."

Are you applying reason to your conflict? Or are you a prisoner of lazy thinking, fear of change, preconceived notions, old news, fake news, or the last loud voice you heard? Across many of life's interactions, the idea of doing a 180-degree turn might make a ton of sense.

- You've been fighting your spouse about installing hardwood floors for years. Maybe it's actually a good idea.
- You love that elm tree on the edge of your property, but really your neighbor should be able to park in his own driveway without getting sap all over his car.
- The elementary school population in your district is declining, so maybe that beloved neighborhood school you've been defending should be closed.
- Your business partner has long been pushing to offer product online. What have you been waiting for?

In truth, there are very few things that don't change or shouldn't change. While God is eternal and immutable, everything on Earth is temporary. So let's all pledge to stay open-minded when it comes to making a well-informed U-turn.

Let's be honest. You picked up this book to uncover strategies for winning arguments. When facing conflict, conventional wisdom suggests the goal is to crush your enemies with clear logic and quiet conviction. Quoting the sixteenth president again, in some cases, there may be an even better strategy. "Am I not destroying my enemies when I make friends with them?"

Application

Less conflict sounds nice, doesn't it? There are a variety of ways to make that happen. You could hide under a rock, avoiding human interaction. You could smite all your foes with a weapon of mass extinction. You could debate them or love them over to your way of thinking. But the option most of us rarely consider might be the easiest: change your own way of thinking.

We're not talking about change for the sake of change. We're talking about listening to all sides of a debate and applying our best decision-making skills to the question or challenge.

A smart, thoughtful, accomplished person (such as yourself) is on target with your thinking 98 percent of the time. Still, that leaves a few rare occasions when the right thing to do is change your mind. The Serenity Prayer, written by Reinhold Niebuhr almost a century ago, comes to mind and still applies. "God, grant me the serenity to accept the things I cannot change, courage to change the things I can, and wisdom to know the difference."

Strategy

Promise yourself this. In the midst of your next several conflicts, pause momentarily to consider, *Might I be wrong and they be right?*

That's all, just ask the question. Then proceed with confidence that comes from conviction.

ESCALATE

By seeing your adversary only as the bad guy. By remaining obstinate even when offered a reasonable course of action that might be worth consideration. By being purely selfish.

DE-ESCALATE

Imagine the possibility that the other party might be offering logic, experience, fresh data, or reasonable motivation for their way of thinking. Flip-flopping and taking their side offers instant and complete de-escalation.

THE BRIDEZILLA EXCEPTION:
One-time allowances for irregular conflicts

Sometimes the proper response to conflict is to let your "adversary" just keep dishing it out. That's right. In extraordinarily rare instances, your job is to smile and accept their ridiculous, exhausting, petty, impossible demands.

Allow me to take this instruction to the point of absurdity. If you're a close friend or relative to the conflict instigator, your responsibility is actually to do everything in your power to make them blissfully happy and assure them that everything is fine. Even if the offender turns into a fussbudget, nitpicker, or barbarian, your role is to continue to do their bidding. Instantly and without question.

Let's call this the "Bride Exemption."

It would be nice if brides took into consideration the needs and feelings of every member of the wedding party and every guest at her wedding. Many brides (and grooms) do exactly that. Let's give them all the credit in the world. Actually, most brides start that way. Upon their engagement, they sincerely believe that all the pieces will fall into place for a lovely, memorable, affordable wedding. A meaningful ceremony. Happy guests. No hurt feelings. A beautiful weekend. All on budget. But about six weeks before the nuptials, the enormity of the task shatters the illusion, and she turns into the proverbial bridezilla that has become a common theme in movies, television, social media, and can be viewed regularly at your own local church and wedding venues near and far.

Here's the point. Don't fight it. Embrace it. Let the bride have her way. Let the bride have her day. Because—and this is important—it's a one-time event. Plus, you never know who or what is influencing her. It may be unspoken, but she is trying to keep a slew of people happy including her mom and dad, her future in-laws, grandparents, old and new BFFs, siblings, a crazy aunt, step-parents and half-siblings, and her husband-to-be.

Her job is not easy. Under a microscope, a bride is planning a fashion show, floral exhibit, photo shoot, vacation, and the biggest party ever. Plus pre-parties and post-parties. There may be toasts to make, dances to learn, reservations to confirm, and jitters to squelch. The deadline is immovable. That date has been printed on save-the-date magnets and fancy invitations for months. Don't forget, the bride also has decades of visions in her own head regarding the perfect wedding. That's a lot to live up to.

Most importantly, let's all remember it's a spiritual event—a sacrament—in which two become one. If you're a true friend or loving family member, you will do anything you can to minimize the stress and pressure in order to give the bride and groom a decent chance to appreciate the sacredness of the moment.

If you perceive a bit of conflict leading up to a wedding, don't be surprised and please don't add fuel to the fire. Deflect hard feelings. Encourage others in your circle to set aside their own ignored preferences or petty vexations. On her wedding day, the bride doesn't need to hear about your botched hotel reservation, the off-key soloist at church, the rude valet, the gristled prime rib, or the long-standing feud you've had with one of your tablemates. And you know what? Even if you mention it an entire year later, you shouldn't expect an apology. So why bring it up?

If a normally wonderful young woman turns into bridezilla for a couple days or even a few weeks, let it go. Maybe even try to appreciate the lighter side of the dilemma. Encourage others also to excuse a bride on her day. What a gift that would be. The bride may never even realize how generous you've been, but that's also okay.

This idea of a one-time exemption from holding individuals accountable for lamentable behavior extends to a handful of other circumstances as well. For example, anything a new mom says to her husband in a delivery room should be instantly forgiven. Unfortunately, many other situations are more dire or disheartening.

For example, when a loved one dies suddenly—a child, sibling, best friend, or parent—all kinds of emotions come to the surface. Even with the best intentions, there may be hurtful words spoken. Let that go. Don't add conflict to grief.

In a hospital room emotions often run high. Words meant to bring comfort sometimes do just the opposite. Let it go. The person speaking those words probably meant well; they just didn't think it through.

When someone in your life endures a significant tragedy— bankruptcy, a hostile divorce, a hate crime, suicide of a loved one, sexual assault, a rebellious teenager—that person may express ideas and thoughts counter to what you believe. Even if you think you have the right words to "correct their thinking," please don't. For now, there's already plenty of conflict in their lives. The better choice is compassion. Or, if you can muster it, empathy. Frankly, even after the wounded party has gone through the many stages of grief, the best you can do is make yourself available with nonjudgmental words of encouragement, love, and gentle guidance.

This chapter contains the mostly manageable—and sometimes amusing—predicament of how to deal with a bridezilla at an occasion that's mostly celebratory. Then the strategy turned the corner to apply to more formidable life-and-death challenges, demonstrating that life inevitably has ups and downs.

With that in mind, perhaps the greatest value of these paragraphs is to serve as a reminder that we don't always know what's going on in the lives of friends, loved ones, acquaintances, and neighbors. If an individual you know fairly well is causing a conflict by acting in a way that's quite atypical, you would do well to consider it a one-time exception.

Application

You have the power to start conflicts and the power to stop them. But sometimes your greatest power is actually stopping conflicts *before* they even start. That's especially the right choice when any conflict revolves around a rare or once-in-a-lifetime event.

I know of too many lifelong hostilities between family members and longtime friends that began during times of high stress, fear, confusion, or loss. Those relationships were completely non-adversarial until one individual made a remark or took action without thinking it through. But here's the application of this strategy: The first thoughtless remark didn't doom the relationship. It was the *response* to that remark that escalated the spark into a decades-long conflagration. The individual undergoing the stressful situation—the bride, grieving parent, or victim—wasn't given the benefit of the doubt, and a feud that never needed to happen was born.

Many conflicts could be avoided altogether if only we took the time to discern what the offending party is currently going through. Especially when we're a little off our game, we all say or do dumb things we regret. Wouldn't it be nice if the person or persons on the receiving end of our blunder readily let us off the hook?

At weddings and funerals and everyplace in between, let's all pledge to try to choose our words more carefully while at the same time realizing that others may be having difficulty choosing their own words. The Bible confirms the difficulty of taming the tongue.

> No human being can tame the tongue. It is a restless evil, full of deadly poison. With the tongue we praise our Lord and Father, and with it we curse human beings, who have been made in God's likeness. Out of the same mouth come praise and cursing. My brothers and sisters, this should not be. (James 3:8–10)

In moments of high emotion, we praise and curse. Sometimes loudly. Sometimes unforgettably. Often unintentionally. It's a shame when good people let those temporary words degenerate into permanent conflict. It's especially heartbreaking among family members or longtime friends.

Strategy

When entering a situation with high emotions, watch for signs and be ready to make allowances for any words or actions that could possibly turn into a longtime feud. It's a one-time exemption. If that individual repeatedly and intentionally shreds you with nasty words or actions, that's a different story. That conflict may require a different remedy.

ESCALATE

By assuming an attack that is not an attack *is* an attack, and then attacking back. Specifically, assuming the actions of a bride (or groom) reflect who they really are or what they really think.

DE-ESCALATE

Understand that when under stress, humans say stuff they don't mean. Forgive and forget gracefully. Especially at weddings. Best case? Sit back and enjoy the show.

DRAW IN THE SAND:
Bring calm to the conflict

I would say the scene captured in John 8 is a prime example of conflict on the edge of disaster.

In the temple courts, a crowd of people has gathered to hear Jesus teach. A group of Pharisees interrupts, bringing in a woman caught in adultery, to see if they can trick Jesus into contradicting the law. But Jesus responds with a kind of time-out. With a simple action and few words he leads his adversaries to an unmistakable conclusion.

> They put her in front of the crowd. "Teacher," they said to Jesus, "this woman was caught in the act of adultery. The law of Moses says to stone her. What do you say?"

They were trying to trap him into saying something they could use against him, but Jesus stooped down and wrote in the dust with his finger. They kept demanding an answer, so he stood up again and said, "All right, but let the one who has never sinned throw the first stone!" Then he stooped down again and wrote in the dust.

When the accusers heard this, they slipped away one by one, beginning with the oldest, until only Jesus was left in the middle of the crowd with the woman. Then Jesus stood up again and said to the woman, "Where are your accusers? Didn't even one of them condemn you?"

"No, Lord," she said. And Jesus said, "Neither do I. Go and sin no more." (John 8:3–11 NLT)

What was Jesus tracing in the sand? The sins of the accusers? Their names? The exact wording of the Old Testament law? Perhaps He created a temporary drawing in the dust that evoked a deeper truth about sin, guilt, and humanity's need for grace.

Jesus did not fall into the trap of the scribes and Pharisees. His strategy is one you and I can use. He listened, carefully measured His words, spoke a single, thought-provoking sentence, and gave His audience time to think it through. It was the compelling silence that led the Pharisees to begin walking away.

Too often, in any kind of debate, the person who talks the longest and loudest loses. Blowhards may generate more sound bites and even get cheers from the crowd, but their words are hollow and miss the mark. Those who take in all the facts, consider what's best for all involved, and offer a reasoned response almost always get their point across more effectively.

It's worth noting that the Bible translation above includes an exclamation mark at the end of Jesus's statement, "All right, but let the one who has never sinned throw the first stone!" I am no biblical scholar, but I don't think He would have been emphatic with His words. I imagine Jesus using a prudent, rational, deliberate tone. Don't you?

Also worth noting is that the oldest Pharisee was the first to leave the scene. That may suggest that thoughtfulness and self-restraint is more likely to accompany age and experience. The younger accusers may have been more eager to start throwing rocks. In your own conflicts, you may need to take into account the age of your adversary.

Beyond conflict with the Pharisees, Jesus had a different kind of conflict with the woman. As an adulterer, she had broken God's laws. Curiously, He chose not to condemn her. But He also didn't ignore what she had done. With clarity, Jesus did say, "Go and sin no more."

We don't know what Jesus traced in the sand and we have no authority to condemn sinners. But we do have the ability to bring calm to an explosive situation. That's a powerful tool in any conflict.[1]

Application

Poise is such a valuable and rare commodity. Composure and discretion provide you time to remind yourself of what you really want and weigh the risks. Slowing things down—drawing in the sand—also gives the other person time to consider their position. You may think that's a bad thing. Why would I want

---

[1] Adapted in part from *What If God Wrote Your To-Do List?* (pp. 128–130), ©2018 by Jay Payleitner, Harvest House Publishers. Used with permission.

to give my adversary time to organize their thoughts and forge their arguments? Remember, especially if it's a long-term relationship, you want them to feel like their needs are being considered. A lasting resolution is virtually impossible unless that happens.

Engendering a slowed-down negotiation process is especially important if you feel like you are being pulled into a trap like the one the Pharisees were plotting. Sometimes you have to say, "Let me get back to you" or "I need to run this past a few people." Put the clock on your side, not theirs. In most cases those offers that are "limited time only" will still be available tomorrow.

Rushing through decisions often leads to bad decisions. Even if the right decision is made, second-guessing often leads to one or both sides pondering, *Did we go too fast? Did we consider all the options?*

Are you caught in a conflict that feels like it's all going too fast? In most cases, you have the right and responsibility to slow things down. Plus, when your own pharisaical thoughts start creeping in, you may want to consider taking the time to stop, lean over, and trace your own fingers in the dust.

Strategy

The very word "conflict" has an edge that puts people in a state of panic and exasperation. Perhaps the opposite of conflict is not resolution, but calm. Fewer words, slower speech, more thoughtfulness, and more time allow everyone to get on the same page and minimize second-guessing.

Infuse your next altercation with poise and composure, and you'll be well on your way to that win you so richly deserve.

ESCALATE

By rushing to judgment. By falling into negotiation traps. By being intimidated by authority figures. By modeling negotiation strategies after the Pharisees'.

DE-ESCALATE

If negotiations are going too fast, call a time-out. Use fewer and more carefully chosen words. Draw in the sand.

HEED ADVICE FROM THE KID NEXT DOOR:
Healing conflicts from years past

Do you partake in the annual ritual of watching *Home Alone* every Christmas? If so, thanks to the writing of John Hughes and the direction of Chris Columbus, you've witnessed one of the most dramatic movie conflicts of all time, complete with a heartwarming resolution.

No, I'm not referring to Kevin McCallister's battle to defend his home from the Wet Bandits. The most important conflict resolved in that 1990 movie occurred next door on the snowy sidewalk leading up to Old Man Marley's house. Don't let Macaulay Culkin's facial expressions, the slapstick pratfalls of Joe Pesci and Daniel Stern, or John Williams's sublime score distract you from the dramatic reconciliation between an older father and his adult son in the very last scene.

Early in the now-classic film, Kevin's older brother, Buzz, menacingly describes Old Man Marley as a serial killer with a snow shovel. But later, Kevin learns the real reason his neighbor lives like a hermit, and offers the older gentleman some innocent and obvious advice.

Let's take a look at that scene, in which Kevin finds himself drawn to a big stone church. The choir is singing in the candlelight. He enters, sits in a pew, and is surprised to see Old Man Marley across the aisle. The man stands and crosses over to where Kevin is seated. Initially, Kevin expresses fear, then confusion as the old man smiles and offers a friendly greeting. They strike up a conversation, and then Old Man Marley asks Kevin if he's been a good boy this year.

KEVIN

I've been kind of a pain lately. I said some things I shouldn't have. I really haven't been too good this year.

OLD MAN MARLEY

Yeah.

KEVIN

I'm kind of upset because I really like my family, even though sometimes I say I don't. Sometimes I even think I don't. Do you get that?

OLD MAN MARLEY

I think so. How you feel about your family is a complicated thing.

KEVIN

Especially with an older brother.

OLD MAN MARLEY

Deep down, you'll always love him. But you can forget that you love him. You can hurt them, and they can hurt you. That's not just because you're young. You want to know the real reason why I'm here right now?

                    KEVIN
Sure.

                OLD MAN MARLEY
I came to hear my granddaughter sing. And I
can't come hear her tonight.

                    KEVIN
You have plans?

                OLD MAN MARLEY
No. I'm not welcome.

                    KEVIN
At church?

                OLD MAN MARLEY
You're always welcome at church. I'm not welcome with my son. Years back, before you and
your family moved on the block, I had an argument with my son.

                    KEVIN
How old is he?

                OLD MAN MARLEY
He's grown up. We lost our tempers, and I said
I didn't care to see him anymore. He said the
same, and we haven't spoken to each other since.

                    KEVIN
If you miss him, why don't you call him?

                OLD MAN MARLEY
I'm afraid if I call that he won't talk to me.

Pretty solid logic from an eight-year-old. "If you miss him, why don't you call him?" Later, just before the credits roll, we see evidence that Old Man Marley has taken that advice. Kevin is drawn to the window where he sees that grandfather hugging his little red-haired granddaughter. Through Kevin's window, the two new friends exchange waves.

The final dialogue of the movie comes from Buzz yelling, "Kevin! What did you do to my room?" and suggests that life will soon be back to chaotic normalcy in the McCallister house. But that's okay. Thanks to Kevin's innocent and childlike prompting, the long-standing conflict next door has been resolved and a family restored.

When you first picked up this book, I'm not sure what conflict or conflicts you were hoping to negotiate or overcome. But if you're part of a prolonged squabble between family members or onetime close friends, this chapter—with its simple, childlike advice—may be worth your consideration.

Application

If you know the film, you should be nodding at this message. If you're not tracking, then I apologize and recommend a viewing of *Home Alone* with someone you love next Christmas. It's a rare movie that's entertaining for all ages.

Of course, we don't know what was said on the phone call between Old Man Marley and his son. We imagine a big dramatic apology, but maybe not! Maybe just hearing the voice of a loved one and a gentle statement suggesting that "I'm sorry about what happened between us" is all it takes. That's a little scary at any age. But it's worth the risk. As Kevin says later in the scene, "At least you'll know."

                        KEVIN
My point is, you should call your son.

                    OLD MAN MARLEY
What if he won't talk to me?

                        KEVIN
At least you'll know. Then you could stop
worrying about it. Then you won't have to be
afraid anymore. I don't care how mad I was,
I'd talk to my dad. Especially around the
holidays.

As you replayed this scene in your mind, did some broken relationship of your own come to mind? Do you have their phone number? Or email address? You know what to do. At the very least, consider reaching out and say, "I was thinking about you" or "It's been a long time and I'm hoping to reconnect. How are you?"

You don't even have to wait for the holidays.

Strategy

Consider the possibility that your son, daughter, mom, dad, brother, sister, or old friend has been thinking about you. What was that fight about anyway? Might time have healed that wound? Not to minimize an interaction or altercation that was truly malicious, but people do change. Now that you're a bit older and wiser, maybe you realize you do have something to apologize for. It's no fun to live with regrets and broken relationships. In some cases, a single two-minute phone call can resolve a decades-long conflict. That call could open the door to much-needed healing or more joy-filled holidays.

ESCALATE

By allowing old wounds to fester. By succumbing to fear. By not placing value on your own life and those who have been part of it.

DE-ESCALATE

Forgive them. Forgive yourself. Hope for the best. Take the chance. Make the call.

EARN THE RIGHT TO SAY WHAT NEEDS TO BE SAID:
Conflicts with your teenager

What relationship is more prone to conflict than that between parents and teenagers?

All the old parenting tricks from when your kids were in elementary school are no longer effective. You really can't lecture, threaten, con, spank them, or send them to their room. You have wisdom to impart, but they think they know it all. You're still responsible for providing for their needs and protecting them from the world, but they are well on their way to spreading their wings and leaving the nest. (Which, by the way, is a good thing.)

You might say their job is to test their limits—to see how much they can get away with. In response, your job is to help them find the safe and sane place to draw that line.

A good friend of mine experienced that exact conundrum with his thirteen-year-old daughter. She was a lovely, well-behaved girl, and they had a great relationship. When he shared an opinion or expectation, she abided by his wishes. It wasn't difficult. He was never unreasonable and she always agreed with his directives. That is, until the warm spring morning she bounced down the hallway steps and was about to head out the front door to the school bus waiting at the end of the driveway.

My friend, in a brief moment of surprise, found himself saying these words: "I can't let you go to school like that. Your shorts are too short."

What was her response? Can you guess?

After the briefest hesitation, she got on the bus and went to school.

If you're a parent—or were ever a teenager—you can probably relate to that moment. In his mind, that dad was saying something his daughter needed to hear. Something that had to be said.

To be clear, this was not a part-time father who showed up one morning to cast judgment and aspersions on a young teen's fashion choices. This was a dad who had been pouring love, faith, creativity, integrity, and wisdom into his daughter's heart and mind for thirteen years. He had talked with her about the value of modesty. He had talked about boys and how they think. He had talked about inner beauty, sexual purity, and setting personal standards.

But he had not talked specifically about the length of blue jean shorts. As a matter of fact, as she left the house she found her father's words confusing. She liked the shorts, it was a nice day, and she wasn't trying to make any kind of statement.

On the other hand, her father thought he had failed her, he had failed the boys who would be lusting after his daughter all day, and he had failed God.

He thought back over his years spending time with her. *Where did I go wrong?* They had always been on the same page. He had listened, delivered biblical truth, told stories from his own youth, and sacrificed to be there for her. He had promised to protect her, and she was glad about that.

Then came the morning she headed out the door in shorts that were too short. And he risked it all. This was not a fictional moment far into the future. This was right now, a split-second decision. This was one of those moments of truth that require great courage from a dedicated father.

My friend did not embarrass his daughter in front of her peers. He did not yell or chase the bus down the street. He did not grab her and force her back into the house. He directly spoke truth into her life. And she got on the bus anyway.

The father and daughter did not speak that evening. After a couple of days, their relationship returned to its previous state. Polite dinner table conversation, coordinating schedules, a clarification about homework, a comment on current events, a laugh over a television show, and a return to the bedtime ritual of prayers and wishes and goodnight kisses.

The incident that morning was never mentioned. From the outside looking in, dad and daughter were once again on the same page.

By the way: she never wore those shorts again.

Also, a sticky note appeared on her full-length bedroom mirror. It was a note she had written herself. It said, "Does what you see honor God?"

A moment of courage on the part of a dedicated father helps a young teen come to a new understanding of her true value in God's eyes. He said what needed to be said and—in the end—their relationship was stronger because of it, and that young woman came to her own personal moment of truth.[2]

---

[2] Adapted in part from *52 Things Daughters Need from Their Dads* (pp. 23–24), ©2013 by Jay Payleitner, Harvest House Publishers. Used with permission.

The only reason that altercation didn't blow up into a shouting match, an embarrassing scene in their driveway, or longtime feud is because that father had earned the right to speak truth into her life.

Application

There are a gazillion parenting books out there. I know, I've written several myself. Expecting to boil parenting advice down to a simple handful of protocols would be impossible, but let me try anyway: Earn trust. Build respect. Laugh together. Set them up for success. Love unconditionally.

Do those things over a long enough period of time and there's a good chance you have earned the right to speak truth into their lives. The truth about right and wrong. The truth about money, sex, drugs, and other temptations. The truth about God's plan for them.

This principle extends to other relationships, but only those that have gone through years of building trust and respect, or perhaps have undergone some cataclysmic experience that creates that kind of bond.

Mentors can do the same for their charges, and a good boss might earn the right to speak with honesty and conviction to a longtime employee. At the end of a fulfilling school year, a committed and creative teacher may have a select student or two with whom they have made that kind of connection. In wartime, a commanding officer expecting to lead troops through hell needs to develop an abundance of trust and respect. Coaches that mold athletes and get the best out of their entire team do so only by knowing their players' strengths and weaknesses and earning the right to speak truth.

As my friend discovered, parents or authority figures have to develop their own convictions before passing them on. Also, you can't share the great truths of life before that trusting relationship has been secured, and you can't do it all at once. When a point of conflict arises, the goal is to deliver well-thought-out information that applies to that circumstance. But sometimes you may be forced to think on your feet. That's when you'll be especially glad your belief system is in place and your relationship is well established.

The Bible confirms that integrity can and should be passed on, and even suggests a benefit for speaking your convictions with care. "Encourage the young men to be self-controlled. In everything set them an example by doing what is good. In your teaching show integrity, seriousness and soundness of speech that cannot be condemned, so that those who oppose you may be ashamed because they have nothing bad to say about us" (Titus 2:6–8).

If your connection is fragile, then attempting to speak into someone's life is a perilous mission destined to end in conflict. But being a parent, mentor, manager, teacher, or coach who has proven to be caring, committed, and available leads to conflicts that will be short-lived and probably valuable experiences. As a result, that next generation will be able to ask themselves the tough questions and make their own well-thought-out decisions.

Strategy

Parents, don't believe the rumors. Every season of your children's lives can actually bring you closer and bring you more personal satisfaction, because every year you're deepening trust and respect. As you love them unconditionally and prepare them for the world, you're earning the right to pass on your convictions. You may even look forward to a little conflict along the way because it leads to great conversations.

Worth mentioning is the fact that cultivating trust and respect is a strategy for reducing and alleviating conflict in all relationships.

ESCALATE

By raising kids with an iron fist without considering their unique gifts, perspectives, desires, hopes, and dreams. By assuming your position of authority automatically entitles you to respect and trust.

DE-ESCALATE

Invest in that loving relationship with your kids early and often. My friend Josh McDowell often said, "Rules without relationship lead to rebellion." Expect teens to test your boundaries. Expect healthy debates. Expect to stay close.

IMAGINE HOW GOD WILL USE YOU:
Conflict as training from a hero's perspective

It's impossible to imagine the physical, emotional, and spiritual turmoil the young Harriet Tubman endured after being born into slavery.

At age six, Harriet was forced to stay awake through the night to care for her master's infant and rock its cradle; if the baby woke, Harriet would be whipped. Harriet's work included wading through freezing marshes to check muskrat traps. As she grew older, Harriet worked the plantation by driving oxen, plowing, and hauling logs.

Somehow, God used it all. As an enslaved person, Harriet lived in fear of being separated from her family. She witnessed her mother's tears as four siblings were sold away in chains. When she was twenty-nine, Harriet also was committed for sale. She ran instead.

Undoubtedly, her lifelong hardships and experiences equipped her for that first journey to freedom. Traveling the "Underground Railroad" meant long sleepless nights and hiding out in marshes between sheltering at safe houses.

Finally, when she gained freedom, her elation was tempered by the knowledge that so many of her loved ones had lost their lives or were still in bondage. Soon thereafter, she dedicated her life to helping free others. Over the next decade, Harriet—now called "Moses" because of her great rescues—helped scores of enslaved people escape, including many of her own family members. Later, she served as a nurse, scout, and spy for the Union Army during the Civil War, and was an activist in the women's suffrage movement.

Comparing any conflict you might be facing with the experiences of Harriet "Moses" Tubman may seem a bit presumptuous, but the point is valid. The adversity she endured prepared her to do great things. So might your conflicts be preparing you for larger-than-life achievements.

Harriet Tubman once said, "Every great dream begins with a dreamer. Always remember you have within you the strength, the patience, and the passion to reach for the stars, to change the world."

Perhaps your own dream and a plan for achieving it will be revealed not by avoiding conflict, but by facing it head-on with courage and fortitude.[3]

---

[3] For detailed information on Harriet Tubman, see Kate Clifford Larson's excellent book, *Bound for the Promised Land: Harriet Tubman, Portrait of an American Hero* (New York: Ballantine Books, 2004).

Application

You didn't pick this book up expecting to find the lesson saying, "Conflicts can be good things!" But of course they can. Examples are easy to come up with.

A sales rep is on the chopping block because she fails to uncover the unspoken needs of a client and blows the deal. Given one more chance, she does a better job of qualifying the next lead and lands an even bigger account.

A high school teacher warns a student he or she is on track to fail the class. That's when the student finally gets serious and realizes his passion for that subject, thereby finding a college major and a career.

A baseball coach is furious with his team because of a litany of mental mistakes that led to a one-run loss to their crosstown rival. After the game, as usual, both teams take a knee in the outfield. One coach spends less than a minute congratulating his team before inviting them all to Dairy Queen. The coach of the losing team spends twenty minutes pointing out specific ways to improve and makes sure their next few practices are focused and productive. Motivated by the desire to resolve that conflict, guess which team wins the next time those rivals square off again?

Muhammad Ali made Joe Frazier better, Larry Bird made Magic Johnson better, and Chris Evert made Martina Navratilova better. And vice versa.

A popular trope in youth fiction, after-school specials, and coming-of-age movies is a middle school kid who finally finds the courage to stand up to the local bully. After the epic scuffle, the two become best friends. It might be a bit corny, but the moral is clear: opposition makes you stronger.

Successfully facing conflicts—whether they are with a slave owner, irate boss, no-nonsense teacher, frustrated coach, archrival, or seventh-grade bully—often requires you to dig deep and do stuff you never thought you could do. To reach for the stars. In many endeavors, putting forth your best effort is not a requirement until you're facing unavoidable conflict. How you respond to those trials makes all the difference.

The Bible challenges us to "Consider it pure joy, my brothers, when you encounter trials of many kinds, because you know that the testing of your faith produces perseverance" (James 1:2–3).

I can't imagine young Harriet Tubman finding joy in her tragic circumstances. Yet historians tell us in her youth she sang the spirituals "Go Down Moses" and "Bound for the Promised Land." Later, she sang those same hymns, secretly changing tempo in the song as a covert signal to her friends and family that it was time to slip away on their grueling journey to freedom.

Strategy

You may be tempted to avoid conflict at all costs. Instead, lean in and see where that conflict leads. Allow it to sharpen you. Listen to a mentor, to your adversary, and to your heart. Maybe it's true that "what doesn't kill you makes you stronger." Surviving today—learning from it—just might put you in position to do great things tomorrow.

ESCALATE

By feeling sorry for yourself. By giving up. By letting anger get the best of you. By being envious of those who seem to have it easy.

DE-ESCALATE

Recognize that trials are part of life. Acknowledge that you may not see the benefit of today's conflict, but God's good plan is still in place. Treat every experience as an investment for the long haul.

Claim Romans 8:28: "In all things God works for the good of those who love him, who have been called according to his purpose."

ESCAPE THE ECHO CHAMBER:
Seek conflict to be your best self

If you're the top dog—large and in charge—you might think your days of dealing with conflict within your organization are over. As boss, no matter the size of your company, association, or ministry, what you say goes. If a subordinate disagrees with you, they're gone. If a client or vendor rubs you the wrong way, they're cut off. As an authoritative parent, if a teenager starts to tell you why your rules are unfair, you send them to their room or ship them off to boarding school.

When you establish that kind of environment, even if people don't agree with you, they pretend they do. As a result, you may tend to feel pretty swell about yourself and your ideas. Cavalier even. You may be tempted to move ahead with every single one of your plans without any hesitation, even if it isn't fully reviewed or researched. There will be no second-guessing and no thoughtful pushback.

How does that sound? Well, because you're a bright person, you would soon conclude that a little conflict is a good thing.

When we surround ourselves with "yes men" or people who agree with everything we say and do, we pretty much are guaranteed to fall short of God's best plan for our lives. Why? Partly because "two heads are better than one." Partners, colleagues, mentors, and staff with different experiences and education provide a variety of opinions, warnings, alternative viewpoints, and ideas you may not have considered. Also, we should never forget that we live in a fallen world, and our own thought patterns and motivations will never measure up to God's best.

Writing on the topic of leadership, financial guru and publisher Art Rainer warns about the negative effects of living in an *echo chamber*, a conflict-free zone in which only your own ideas are heard and considered. Rainer describes four dangers for leaders whose work environments have become echo chambers.

Good ideas will go unspoken. Echo chambers develop not because of the team's love for their leader, but because of their fear of him or her. While a team member may have a better idea, they do not share it.

Echo chambers perpetuate a team's lack of trust in their leader. As an echo chamber persists, the likelihood of a team member questioning their leader dwindles. And so does the trust in the leader's ability to do what is best for the organization and for each team member.

Echo chambers inflate the leader's ego, making them a worse leader. Leaders in an echo chamber will quickly convince themselves that their ideas are truly best. They will begin to think they have all the answers and are stripped of humility that would lead to any desire to listen, empathize, and grow.

At some point, the flaws will be seen. It won't be the team members that reveal the leader's flaws—it will come from someplace else. A bad decision will be made, and someone from the outside, where there is no fear of the leader, will speak honestly without reservation. The leader will be left wondering how the situation ever got that bad.[4]

If you spend most of your time avoiding conflict or dismissing the advice of anyone who sees things differently, then you really have forfeited your chance to discover the best God has for you.

---

[4] Art Rainer, "4 Dangers of a Leader's Echo Chamber," Ministry Grid, April 28, 2016, https://ministrygrid.com/4-dangers-of-a-leaders-echo-chamber.

To be clear, this chapter is not recommending you intentionally allow conflict to escalate. Just the opposite! If it comes from a trusted source in the form of new ideas and reasonable questions, then embrace the conflict. Even seek it out. Instead of conflict, you'll experience the powerful gift of collaboration. Which, again, is the opposite of escalating conflict.

To execute this strategy, simply try to be aware of anytime you find yourself not being challenged. Family members, friends, teachers, coaches, mentors, pastors, colleagues, even your support staff and your own kids should feel the freedom to say, "Is there a better way?" or "What if we tried this...?"

Application

Have you found yourself in a position or season of life when you were not being challenged? Everything came too easy. Or everyone in your circle of influence was too busy with their own projects to care about yours? That probably meant you weren't doing your best work. It also speaks to the value of teamwork.

Leaders aren't the only ones who find themselves living in an echo chamber. Many of us only read or listen to ideas that match our own. Often, our social circles and social media all echo the same message. We relish the affirmation and begin to believe we already have all the answers. Which means we stop pursuing truth or thinking new thoughts.

In many ways, we do have access to ultimate truth and guidance. As Christians, we have the Bible, the Holy Spirit, prayer, and the wise counsel of mentors, pastors, and accountability partners. But our *interpretation* of what we hear from those sources can be corrupted by the limitations of our earthbound reality. Isaiah 55:8–9 explains it well: "'My thoughts are not your thoughts, neither are your ways my ways,' declares the LORD. 'As the heavens are higher than the earth, so are my ways higher than your ways, and my thoughts than your thoughts.'"

In other words, we need to aspire to have the mind of Christ, but never assume we have achieved it. Anyone who thinks they are 100 percent heavenly minded is probably no earthly good.

Strategy

To escape the echo chamber, we first need to accept the fact that our own voice can lead us astray. We need to stop being smug or self-righteous, because we all still have much to learn. It's very possible that we just need to listen more to the wisdom, experience, and opinions of those around us. Especially those whose voices are sometimes overlooked.

Outside the echo chamber, we will very likely hear someone who disagrees with our point of view, but that's often a good thing. You don't have to change your mind, but you do need to hear them out.

Or maybe the lesson here is to stop blowing smoke or kissing up to someone in authority. You are doing them no favors. And your own wisdom and experience is being wasted.

ESCALATE

By assuming you have all the answers. By closing yourself off to the viewpoints of others. By not speaking up when you have something that needs to be heard.

DE-ESCALATE

Allow humility and curiosity to open the door to fresh winds and inspirations. Be a respectful teammate by sharing and receiving insights. Have an open-door policy for new ideas and respectful pushback.

THE INSTANT SINCERE APOLOGY:
Curtail conflict on the spot

We've got great neighbors. I wouldn't trade them for anything, even though we're not always on the same page. Their grass is greener than mine. Their kids were less boisterous than ours. During an election, any campaign signs in front of our two homes indicate we're probably cancelling out each other's votes. But again, Karen and Vance have always been great neighbors.

I hope you also have great neighbors. Even if you don't, I recommend you do whatever it takes to keep the peace. If nothing else, it opens the door to amusing small talk about the weather, local politics, sports, and marauding raccoons, rattlesnakes, coyotes, moose, or alligators, depending on what part of the country you live in. Plus, make nice with your neighbors, and you can just about always borrow a cup of sugar, jumper cables, or a fertilizer spreader.

With that in mind, allow to me to confirm the benefit of instant and sincere apologies for the purpose of avoiding long-term conflict.

On a summer evening a couple years ago, my extended family was enjoying our backyard as the sun was just beginning to set. I had the charming idea of extending our time together with a marshmallow roast around our firepit, which had not been fired up in a month or so. I had been collecting twigs, leaves, and pine needles in the firepit for some time, leaving a good-sized pile of kindling.

The fire started easily. You might even call it a burst of flame and smoke. Not a problem, because a light breeze kicked up at just the right time to carry away that surprising cloud. Unbeknownst to me, that smoky cloud headed around the corner of my house and straight into the yard of our dear neighbors, who happened to be entertaining on their screened-in porch. A moment later, six-foot-four Vance stuck his head over our fence, calling out, "Jay, what's going on?" A little surprised and embarrassed, I reverted to my favorite verbal defense mechanism, which happens to be sarcasm. I think I said something not-so-witty about sending smoke signals to the neighborhood.

In short order, the fire had calmed and the smoke had dissipated, and we did roast a few marshmallows and craft a few perfect s'mores. Overall, firing up the firepit was a good decision. Except that I was still a bit embarrassed and now feeling a wee bit guilty about the smoke and my offhand rude response to Vance's legitimate question.

Excusing myself from the firepit conversation, I trudged over to my neighbor's porch and—with authentic sincerity—gave a brief apology. "Hey, I'm really sorry. The smoke and the breeze took me by surprise, I should have known. It was quite a cloud, wasn't it? Again, sorry."

Thankfully, Karen, Vance, and their guests were gracious. Someone did say something about having asthma—which made me feel even worse, but they were just being honest. Case closed.

Looking back, it wasn't really a big deal. And that's the point. If I had not delivered that intentional and timely apology, I'm fairly certain it would have become a bigger deal, and that minor skirmish could have extended through the summer and beyond. Was there a conflict? Yep. At the time, I didn't know how significant it was. And that's also an important point. A conflict that seems petty to you might be a huge deal to your sibling, teammate, customer, neighbor, or anyone with whom you occasionally cross paths. You'll know it's a big deal when that person suddenly gives you the cold shoulder, unfriends you on social media, starts spreading gossip about you, or worse.

Application

We all say and do stupid stuff. The key is to admit it and get past it.

Too often when we hurt someone's feelings or try to minimize the impact of our words or misdeeds, we deflect any responsibility and blame the injured party. We say or think, *They need to toughen up. They need to grow some skin. Life isn't supposed to be easy.* When in actuality, it's us that made the mess and us that should toughen up and do the hard work of apologizing.

The irony is that saying "I'm sorry" is easy. Physically, it takes less than a second and about as much energy as blinking your eyes. Emotionally, it's only difficult if you're three years old and sitting in a sandbox. For some reason, most toddlers don't like to apologize. Maturity allows you to realize that when you mess up, an apology is in order. The only emotion attached to an apology is relief. It's a wonderfully effortless mechanism to go from guilty to guilt-free.

Spiritually, the Bible outlines the clear benefits of making an efficient apology when you do someone wrong. If you sense a dispute rising, stop it before it overflows. "The beginning of strife is like letting out water, so quit before the quarrel breaks out" (Proverbs 17:14).

Consider mastering the art of the prompt, sincere apology. Keep that strategy for instant reconciliation handy—especially in the very early stages of most conflicts. Even if there never were any hard feelings, that apology is not wasted. Moving forward, that person will consider you one of those rare individuals with a big heart and caring disposition. That's not a bad reputation to have.

Take it from someone who messes up a lot: traveling through life is so much easier when you're not walking on eggshells or trying to avoid a bunch of people because you may have unintentionally or unthinkingly ticked them off.

Strategy

This strategy is not difficult at all to explain. If you mess up—even if your blunder disappears in a cloud of smoke—do yourself a favor and deliver a sincere apology as soon as possible. The goal is to clear the air before the conflict gets a chance to grab a foothold. It works with people who are casual acquaintances, neighborly neighbors, very dear, or complete strangers.

ESCALATE

By assuming your gaffes have no consequences. By minimizing the feelings of others. By seeing an apology as a sign of weakness.

DE-ESCALATE

Acknowledge and apologize. Take responsibility for your actions even if the indiscretion was accidental and no one was really harmed.

REACH FOR A NEW LEVEL OF EXCELLENCE:
Embrace conflict as motivation

The 1980s were the glory days of advertising, and I happened to be lucky enough to be right in the middle of it. Every big ad agency had entire floors dedicated to boring stuff like research, production, and account management, but the personality and success of agencies in that era were defined by the creative department—and I was a busy, prolific copywriter.

This was before social media, ROI algorithms, and market segmentation. The actual sales generated by an ad or spot were almost impossible to measure. This was advertising by gut feel. We were building brands with inspired graphics, clever taglines, and big budgets.

In the decade *before* my time in the business, copywriters worked solo, coming up with ideas and then sending them down the hallway for art directors to turn into storyboards or layouts. But in my years in the business—assigned to accounts like Midway Airlines, Kroger Supermarket, and Corona Beer—we worked in two-person teams: one writer and one art director bouncing ideas off each other and deciding which ones to present to a creative director for consideration.

For many copywriters, that became a painful source of conflict. Suddenly, art directors became the gatekeepers for what was presented. For those preliminary storyboards and print layouts, some art directors would frequently sketch and design only their own concepts, not yours. During my time on Michigan Avenue in Chicago, I partnered with more than a dozen art directors, and a few of them would politely nod their head at my suggestions and then quickly say, "Take a look at this," while they sketched out their own graphics and headlines. Before I knew it, we were walking into the creative director's office with three storyboards—none of which were mine.

Working with those slightly stubborn art directors, the only time my concepts were presented was when the ideas were so solid they could not be dismissed. Which meant I had to develop headlines, campaigns, and branding concepts that were undeniably and distinctly inspired.

Guess what happened? I had to up my game. I did my homework. I didn't settle for anything less than a breakthrough idea. I earned a new reputation as a copywriter who could deliver on-target concepts that were short and sweet. That included taglines, positioning statements, jingle lyrics, book titles, posters, even T-shirts. I gained respect from my coworkers and, ultimately, a healthy respect for myself.

Looking back, it was conflict with talented, headstrong art directors that helped make me a better writer. At the time, they ticked me off. But I can trace my current writing skills back to the cutthroat nature of working in those competitive agency creative departments early in my career. That's where I honed my ability to focus and approach challenges from an unexpected angle. And, ultimately, to string together words that bring hope, guidance, and inspiration.

Application

As we've already established, the way you respond to conflict will determine whether you are on a path to loss and despair or moving toward being your best self. If possible, I recommend you make a conscious choice to see your next conflict as motivation for greatness.

Rise above your next conflict. Be ticked off if you need to be. Be better. Prove to the world and to yourself that this challenge will not hold you back. Just the opposite.

Be a better writer or idea generator. Be a better boss or employee. Be a better spouse or parent. Be a better neighbor or hero in the community. Be a better baker, librarian, pastor, nurse, auto dealer, short-order cook, bank teller, news anchor, or floral designer.

When a conflict leaves us feeling as if we have been treated unfairly, sometimes we're so busy feeling sorry for ourselves that we forget that God might be giving us a singular opportunity to overcome that injustice on our own. Working smarter and harder is never a bad option. One of my favorite passages of Scripture reminds us that every project in front of us also comes with the responsibility to put in some sweat equity: "Whatever your hand finds to do, do it with all your might" (Ecclesiastes 9:10).

That Old Testament directive to *do your best* is clear. But what if God knows you could use a little motivation to make that happen? Along with that task at hand, might He include a minor conflict such as the fear of losing your job, cynical words from some naysayer, a competition for recognition, or a botched opportunity that needs repair? Do you see how a conflict can sometimes be a tool God uses to challenge you to kick your efforts up a notch?

Looking back at your own life, you can probably remember when some obstacle that landed in your path led you to think new thoughts and reach new summits of achievement. God bless that obstacle.

Strategy

Consider what work is right in front of you. If you're not doing it "with all your might" then you've created your own conflict. Use that thought as motivation to bring all your tools and skills to the challenge. Don't settle. A little competition (aka a little conflict) in life is often a good thing. That can include competition with a despised adversary, a work colleague, a classmate hoping to edge you out for valedictorian, a teammate vying for your spot in the batting order, or any endeavor in which you can make a decisive decision to "up your own game."

A warning: Track your emotions. Don't let that competition distract you from your more important role as a decent human and follower of Christ.

ESCALATE

By avoiding all conflict because you're afraid to fail or don't want to put in the work. By getting angry at those who have thrown down a gauntlet of challenge. By assuming that good enough is good enough.

DE-ESCALATE

Allow conflict to challenge you to new levels of excellence. Embrace competition or stumbling blocks with courage, creativity, and a vision of what could be. Up your game.

THE CHURCH DIVIDED:
Speak truth into any conflict with eternal implications

I'm not sure what's going on at your church, but there's a good chance a few of the folks sitting in that pew over there are engaging in a bit of a snit with those people sitting over there. At potlucks and prayer services, they may look like they are on the same team, but behind closed doors, nasty words and wrathful thoughts may be taking over.

Conflict in the church is not new. It's actually quite common. Why do you think there are so many denominations? The *World Christian Encyclopedia* actually suggests that the "six major ecclesiastico-cultural mega-blocs" account for more than thirty-three thousand denominations.[5] Critics of Christianity point to that number to argue that a true God would do a better job of communicating and clarifying belief systems with His followers.

But further examination of the numbers would reveal that many of the "denominations" are single, independent churches or smaller enclaves of churches set apart by geography or culture. The core teachings of almost all Christian churches include similar doctrines pertaining to God, Jesus, Holy Spirit, creation, grace, salvation, and so on.

Still, because humans are the ones in leadership, conflicts do crop up within congregations, especially as they add members. The book of Acts famously describes a conflict in the early Church precipitated by an influx of new believers. Gentiles were coming to Christ! But the new converts didn't quite see the value in being circumcised. Jewish Christians came forward insisting it was critical to follow the law of Moses, which meant new members of the Church were expected to become Jewish before being baptized. This was no small showdown.

A recognizable group of first-century church leaders would weigh in on the topic, including Paul, Barnabas, James, and Peter. They took the question seriously and turned not to their own opinions, but to what they previously had heard clearly from God regarding those who had been purified by grace through faith.

The apostles and elders met to consider this question. After much discussion, Peter got up and addressed them: "Brothers, you know that some time ago God made a

---

[5] David B. Barrett, George T. Kurian, Todd M. Johnson eds., *World Christian Encyclopedia, 2nd ed.*(Oxford, et al.: Oxford University Press, USA, 2001), http://www.philvaz.com/apologetics/a106.htm.

choice among you that the Gentiles might hear from my lips the message of the gospel and believe. God, who knows the heart, showed that he accepted them by giving the Holy Spirit to them, just as he did to us. He did not discriminate between us and them, for he purified their hearts by faith. Now then, why do you try to test God by putting on the necks of Gentiles a yoke that neither we nor our ancestors have been able to bear? No! We believe it is through the grace of our Lord Jesus that we are saved, just as they are." (Acts 15:6–11)

After Peter's inspired pronouncement, Barnabas and Paul added their endorsement, confirming that God had been working many miracles among the Gentiles. Then James added a clarification, that while grace was sufficient for the salvation of the new Gentile believers, the law of Moses was still instructive for how they lived.

It is my judgment, therefore, that we should not make it difficult for the Gentiles who are turning to God. Instead we should write to them, telling them to abstain from food polluted by idols, from sexual immorality, from the meat of strangled animals and from blood. For the law of Moses has been preached in every city from the earliest times and is read in the synagogues on every Sabbath. (Acts 15:19–21)

Like so many passages about the early Church, there are multiple lessons for today. One, we should expect occasional conflict between sincere members of any church community. Two, when conflict arises, bring the elders and leaders together. Three, separate opinions from facts and determine the real issue. Four, turn to God's Word. Five, get all parties on the same page. Six, in an effort to unite the opposing parties, reinforce the ideals and goals they have in common.

Bible scholars disagree about the purpose of James's statement that restated a handful of Jewish laws. But I think he was throwing a bone to the Jewish Christians. Peter, Barnabas, and Paul had all taken the side of the Gentile believers. James was just confirming that the debate had been productive, both sides were considered, and the long history of the Jewish people should not be forgotten.

Application

If you're in church leadership, please follow the lead of the first-century Christians and take the concerns of the congregation seriously. The question about circumcision for believers brought together Paul, Barnabas, James, Peter, and a host of other leaders, and they had "much discussion." In recent years, church communities have broken up over issues that were significantly less controversial. As noted above, there are already enough denominations to meet the needs of all.

In churches, denominations, ministries, and other organizations run by Christian principles, there's additional expectation on leaders and elders to be self-disciplined and humble. The Bible describes the character of a Christian leader:

> Now the overseer is to be above reproach, faithful to his wife, temperate, self-controlled, respectable, hospitable, able to teach, not given to drunkenness, not violent but gentle, not quarrelsome, not a lover of money.
> (1 Timothy 3:2–3)

In most conflicts, when one side emerges victorious, it's wise to consider the mindset of the losing side as you move forward. The adage "to the victor belong the spoils" may be true, but that doesn't mean victors should gloat or ignore the needs of their adversaries. Even though the leadership team of the early Church decided circumcision was not a requirement for followers of Christ, James made a point of acknowledging and upholding other Jewish traditions.

Likewise, after a seemingly one-sided victory or decision, it might be wise to remind all those involved that there's value in respectful debate and the opinions brought to the table for discussion.

When it comes to matters of faith, our biggest conflict—how to reconcile the wages of sin—was resolved on the cross. Jesus Himself rescued humanity from our broken condition by choosing to shed His blood and ultimately claim victory over death.

Strategy

In any conflict—especially within a larger group with a purpose greater than itself—honor the concerns and warnings of all the members. Allow the collective wisdom of those in authority—trusting God—to deliberate long enough and have their say. Always be transparent and esteem the value of debate and the integrity of those who shared their concerns.

ESCALATE

By ignoring concerns of certain factions. By being cavalier about throwing out the old in favor of the new. By watching idly as good people pull out and go their own way.

DE-ESCALATE

Welcome input. Bring leaders together. Be transparent. See the value in open-minded debate. Respect opinions. Acknowledge the benefits all members bring to the table.

THE SPORTS CONFLICT PARADOX:
Reversing positive and negative conflict

Did you ever consider there are two extremes when it comes to conflict in the scope of athletics?

With five sports-minded kids, my wife and I found ourselves in the bleachers and sitting on the sidelines at literally hundreds of wrestling matches, football and soccer games, baseball and softball games, and track and field events. We wouldn't trade those experiences for anything. Competitive sports have brought our family closer and taught our kids all kinds of lessons regarding goal-setting, teamwork, leadership, handling disappointment, and other life skills that will serve them well beyond the world of athletics.

Was there conflict on those fields of battle? Yes, absolutely. Wonderful, healthy, spirited, and determined competition.

Were there other conflicts related to those dozens of teams, coaches, referees, and leagues? Yes, regrettably. Without going into detail, I can recall several instances when individuals (including myself) said or thought things that went too far. Conflicts that escalated. These were not proud moments for any coach or parent. (Take heart; apologies have been delivered.)

That experience serves as a reminder of the two kinds of conflict in sports—and in life. There's healthy competition that brings out the best in the participants—let's call that positive conflict.

Then there are regrettable clashes that drag down just about everyone involved. Let's label that negative conflict.

On the surface, those two extremes can be readily identified. Inspiring examples of positive conflict occur in sports, games, clubs, and hobbies that tend to cultivate skills, sharpen the mind, and encourage creativity. In business, positive competition spurs innovation, improves service, lowers prices, and leads to higher-quality products. If you don't keep up, you're out of business. And rightfully so.

Negative conflict might evolve from jealousy, lack of trust, lust, fear, guilt, resentment, miscommunication, perfectionism, or even jumping to conclusions. We've all been there with so many different relationships.

Here's the question: Can those conflicts be reversed? Is it possible to turn negative conflicts into positive conflicts? And perhaps even more daunting, how can we prevent positive conflicts from spiraling into negative experiences?

Let's revisit competition in sports as the laboratory for reversing conflicts in either direction.

When positive conflicts start turning negative, the culprit is often temptation triggered by greed, pride, envy, or some other power grab.

The history of professional baseball contains many instances when our beautiful national pastime turned ugly. That includes players betting on games, as with the 1919 "Black Sox" scandal or Pete Rose's questionable gambling activities in the 1980s. Sadly, the use of steroids has brought skepticism to many power hitting records. Sign-stealing via technology in more recent years has cast a shadow over the Houston Astros and other teams.

While we can applaud aggressiveness and creativity, including jawing with umpires and the old hidden-ball trick, let's all agree that cheating can quickly turn healthy competition into something dishonorable. That's a warning we must heed in any endeavor. If we let down our guard—choosing less than God's best—some important aspect of our lives can turn sour.

In business, manufacturing shortcuts, price gouging, insider trading, false advertising, pyramid schemes, and countless other fraudulent practices can cause a successful enterprise to become a dumpster fire. In relationships, a bit of gossip, a little white lie, a grudge, nitpicking, name-calling, or just taking that other person for granted can turn someone from ally to adversary.

The good news is that negative conflicts can also be reversed. The case studies in these chapters should have given you ammunition to face your next negative conflict with optimism. Applying the Four Factors, along with avoiding the Three Mistakes and not taking the bait to escalate, should have you well on your way to making a U-turn on the negative conflicts you're dealing with now and in the future.

Application

If you're not a fan of baseball, I apologize for the not-so-useful analogy. But the point should be clear. To some, the word "conflict" may instantly trigger negative baggage. It's one of those words to which people assign a value judgment, but they really shouldn't. I think we've made the point several times: conflict can be good or evil, positive or negative.

It's the same with the word "pride." As Christians, we're not supposed be proud. Proverbs 16:18 famously says, "Pride goes before destruction, a haughty spirit before a fall." But if pride comes as a result of overcoming a conflict or digging deep to bring out your best in a competition, I think we should call that *healthy*. A parent surely should take pride when a son pulls up his grade-point average or a daughter brings home a bowling trophy.

Especially after making tough choices to honor God, it's commendable to celebrate. When an alcoholic gets his one-year sobriety chip, he or she may give all the credit to God, but should also take pride in the personal accomplishment.

If you're living the dream by experiencing a positive conflict, congratulations and beware. Enjoy that season. But remember, in trying to stay ahead of the competition or make an extra buck, you may be tempted to skimp on quality or service. Don't do it. In the long run, that'll come back to bite you. If you happen to be a college athlete on scholarship or even a professional athlete receiving a paycheck for playing a kids' game, don't be tempted to juice or cheat in order to make the starting lineup or all-star team. Likewise, if you're a parent—take it from me—don't turn your children's sports competition from positive to negative by being the jerk in the stands.

On the other hand, even after reading the case studies, you may still remain stuck in the middle of a negative conflict. Well, keep reading. The remaining chapters deliver Skills to Build, Tactics and Tricks, and how to see conflict resolution as A Way of Life.

Strategy

Know that you are not the first to struggle with addressing conflict. The right and wrong strategies for claiming victory were established long ago. Proverbs 16:7 is good rule of thumb: "When a man's ways please the Lord, he makes even his enemies to be at peace with him" (ESV).

ESCALATE

By taking the easy way out of conflict. By taking shortcuts, playing dirty, or flirting with temptation. By allowing a positive conflict to turn negative.

DE-ESCALATE

Be steadfast against temptation. Appreciate that when the dust settles on any conflict, God can be glorified. Invite Him to guide you and help you be your best in all your conflicts and competitions.

CHAPTER 6

SKILLS TO BUILD

Good news for everyone you know and love: even as you study up and consider ways to flip, eliminate, and de-escalate conflict, you are actually learning skills that make you a nicer person—or at least easier to live with overall.

Setting aside the Four Factors for a moment, there are life skills you can build and master that will come in handy in marriage, with extended family, on the job, in the community, and in sharing your faith. These are skills you can use even during seasons when you are mostly living free of conflict.

As a matter of fact, the next dozen or so vignettes might even be considered a short course in conflict prevention. Wouldn't it be nice to completely bypass a few of your next ones?

The mechanics of conversation—active listening, using encouraging words, and controlling your body language—are just part of what's ahead. Using humor, working toward win-win solutions, and steering clear of grudges are also profitable life skills. In addition, you'll discover reminders and strategies for being honest with yourself, putting your cards on the table, and getting to the root of conflict.

As you turn these next few pages, don't be surprised if you become a champion for conflict. You may even begin to see it as a learning tool for the next generation or a gateway to the arts.

ACTIVE LISTENING:
First rule of conflict

One legend of the Revolutionary War is the commander at the Battle of Bunker Hill telling his soldiers, "Don't fire until you see the whites of their eyes." He wanted them to preserve their gunpowder until their muskets could do the most damage to the British redcoats. That's good advice.

In battle—especially in 1775 when it took an experienced soldier about thirty seconds to reload—you wanted to make every shot count.

The same principle works in verbal conflicts, and the best way to make every shot count is to listen. Really listen. In almost every argument or debate, the winner is the contender who learns to use their adversary's own words against them. Not throwing them back in their face, but listening to discern their side of the story and then responding with effective and persuasive arguments. It goes back to the idea of empathy.

Of course, entire books have been dedicated to improving your listening skills. If that's an area where you fall short, you may want to do a deep dive into other available resources. But a few bullet points will get you started.

- *Listen to hear, not just to wait for your turn to speak.*
  In our eagerness to share our own brilliance, we turn
  our attention to formulating our own words, and we
  miss out on theirs.
- *Keep an open mind.* Even if the speaker is generally
  off the mark, once in a while they may hit the target
  with a point worth hearing.
- *Don't be an interrupter.* It's rude and unwelcome.
  Better to wait for a pause and then ask permission to
  present your ideas. "Can I share my thoughts on
  that?" will avail you of a more receptive audience than
  "You're wrong and here's why!"
- *Don't feel like you have to fill every silence.*
- *Offer brief affirmations* such as "that makes sense,"
  "that's true," or "good point." Even if you disagree in
  principle, your adversary usually has some ideas that
  have merit.

Active listening is especially important in a debate scenario. By
listening you can sharpen—even weaponize—the words you use,
the defense you make, and the line of reasoning you present. Wasting
your breath and being off target with your reasoning only escalates
the frustration on both sides. You become irate because your adversary is not being persuaded. They're resentful because the arguments
you're making have nothing to do with the real issue. Proverbs 18:13
confirms, "To answer before listening—that is folly and shame."

One strategy for active listening is to keep asking questions
until the other person is forced to reveal his true motivations. Sometimes an adversary doesn't want you to know what they really want.
That means it's up to you to get to the heart of the matter.

In most cases, your adversary does want to be heard. And until you really listen, you have no chance of actually winning the debate. Remember, the argument is not won by the person who speaks the most words, but by the one who uncovers and delivers a resolution that both sides can live with.

Want to win your next verbal battle? Then listen.

USE ENCOURAGING LANGUAGE:
Words add to or subtract from conflict

If the first rule of conflict is active listening, the second might be choosing words that build up, give hope, and bring healing. The Bible has much to say about the power of words and how they are used.

> Like apples of gold in settings of silver is a ruling rightly given. (Proverbs 25:11)

One of the biggest concerns you'll have in any debate or negotiation is how to respond to your adversary's questions or accusations.

> Let your conversation be always full of grace, seasoned with salt, so that you may know how to answer everyone. (Colossians 4:6)

Worth remembering. Our audience is not just our adversary, but God is listening, too.

> May the words of my mouth and the meditation of my heart be pleasing to you, O Lord, my rock and my redeemer. (Psalm 19:14 NLT)

Your words are actually a good indication of the condition of your heart. Cleaning up your speech, though, is more than just a work of your will. It needs to be a work of the Spirit.

> For the mouth speaks what the heart is full of. A good man brings good things out of the good stored up in him, and an evil man brings evil things out of the evil stored up in him. But I tell you that everyone will have to give account on the day of judgment for every empty word they have spoken. For by your words you will be acquitted, and by your words you will be condemned. (Matthew 12:34–37)

So slow down. Think through what you want to say.

> Do you see someone who speaks in haste? There is more hope for a fool than for them. (Proverbs 29:20)

A verse referenced earlier in our case study on conflict in organizations is worth repeating. Paul's words to the church at Ephesus could very well be the overarching theme for this entire book!

> Let no corrupting talk come out of your mouths, but only such as is good for building up, as fits the occasion, that it may give grace to those who hear. (Ephesians 4:29)

Finally, don't beat yourself up when your words get out of control. Instead, take it as a reminder that whether we bless or curse, we are living in the light of God's love. He can heal us. He will make all things right. We just have to ask.

No one can tame the tongue. It is restless and evil, full of deadly poison. Sometimes it praises our Lord and Father, and sometimes it curses those who have been made in the image of God. And so blessing and cursing come pouring out of the same mouth. Surely, my brothers and sisters, this is not right! (James 3:8–10 NLT)

WATCH YOUR TONE AND BODY LANGUAGE:
Conflict beyond words

Words matter. Choose yours wisely. But also be aware that communication and influence is so much more than providing facts and opinions.

In 1971, Albert Mehrabian, a professor at UCLA, published research suggesting 93 percent of a speaker's message is non-verbal.[1] Initially touted as the "7 percent rule," that notion has been refuted over the years. Still, there's reason to believe body language and tone of voice have more impact than you might realize.

Is it a coincidence that the year in which COVID-19 shut down human interaction and masked our smiles was also the year when hate, division, and violence escalated beyond our imagination? I don't think so.

Consider the ramifications of being forced to mumble through masks and endure two-dimensional Zoom calls with distorted audio. I think you'll agree those are not unifying methods of communication. That unsettling period is clear evidence of the critical need we have for handshakes, hugs, human touch, smiles, eye contact, and even small talk and warm wishes.

---

[1] Philip Yaffe, "The 7% Rule: Fact, Fiction, or Misunderstanding," *Ubiquity* 2011 (October 2011), https://doi.org/10.1145/2043155.2043156.

With that goal in mind, let's consider some of the universal principles taught in business schools regarding non-verbal communication. In most situations, your goal is to put your adversary at ease. (Although, knowledge of these techniques can also be used to vex your adversary or put them on the defensive.)

- Make eye contact. But avoid the bug-eyed stare down.
- Smile. But not too big.
- Sit up. Avoid slouching.
- Gesture with open hands. But not too broadly.
- With hands rested on a desk or table, keep your fingertips lightly touching.
- Avoid crossing your arms, unless you want to appear defiant.
- Turn toward the person speaking.
- Lean in to conversations.
- Nod occasionally, maybe even give a brief three-nod affirmation. But avoid continual, exaggerated head bobbing.
- Steer clear of clichéd gestures such as thumbs up, crossed fingers, or the OK sign. (In addition to being clichéd, many common hand gestures deliver offensive messages in other countries.)

Mirroring is a body-language principle to be used with care. While talking to someone one-on-one, if they tilt their head or lean back in their chair, simply do the same. You can even gain rapport by mirroring the way they stand, crossing your legs to reflect their sitting posture, matching their breathing, raising your eyebrows, and matching other facial expressions. Some of this comes naturally. But if you find yourself mimicking, you'll want to ease off. If you overdo mirroring and get caught, you could jeopardize your relationship.

Also, be very careful entering the personal space of an acquaintance or adversary. Avoid "close talking," which can be unnerving. Unless again, your goal is to make the other person uncomfortable.

Your speaking tone is all about cadence, volume, timbre, inflection, and articulation. As indicated above, how you say something can be just as important as what you say. Any phrase—"The meeting is at 10 *a.m.*"—can be hostile, helpful, accusatory, judgmental, deferential, or dutiful based on all those tonal factors, especially considering which word is emphasized.

You can choose to use a tone that wounds or one that heals. Proverbs 12:18 reminds us, "The words of the reckless pierce like swords, but the tongue of the wise brings healing."

APPLY HUMOR:
Conflict can't stand up to laughter

In the middle of a heated debate or serious conflict I typically do not recommend pausing for a knock-knock joke. Nor would I suggest turning to sarcasm, potty humor, practical jokes, or slapstick comedy. But laughter is universal and, if you can pull it off, comedy could be a valuable skill to add to your de-escalation toolbox.

Earlier, we explored some of the history surrounding the 1962 Cuban missile crisis. Reportedly, humor played a significant role in de-escalating the potential disaster. Russia was preparing to install nuclear missiles in Cuba—ninety miles off the Florida coast—and President Kennedy was determined to block the construction. In the

midst of a tense confrontation between American and Soviet representatives, a Russian delegate stood up and told a joke: "What is the
difference between Capitalism and Communism? In Capitalism,
man exploits man. In Communism, it is the other way around." The
tension eased, talks resumed, and World War III was avoided.[2]

If you've been in one industry for a while, you know that inside
jokes are common, especially with clients, suppliers, and competitors you've known for a while. A little satirical or cynical humor
may serve you well when your longtime supplier suddenly hits you
with a major price increase. Feel free to respond with an off-handed
threat to take your business elsewhere. Maybe even name that one
supplier known throughout the industry for shoddy workmanship:
"A 15 percent price increase? I just may have to take my business
to Schnook Industries."

That kind of humor acknowledges that you've heard their offer,
but you are expecting them to sharpen their pencil. You really
wouldn't buy from "Schnook Industries," but you wouldn't hesitate
to shop around.

Another example might be that longtime employee who comes
your office looking for a raise. You do have a little money in your
budget, so you offer to give them half the amount they request.
Then, not in a mean-spirited way, but with slightly sardonic
delivery, suggest they have another option: "If that's not enough,
word on the street is they're hiring over at Blockbuster." (Or Sears.
Or Pan Am. Or Myspace. Or Edsel.) That employee will get the
joke and take your offer.

---

[2] Karen Buxman, "Humor as a Negotiation Tool—or—How Humor Saved the
World," LinkedIn, November 2, 2016, https://www.linkedin.com/pulse/
humor-negotiation-toolorhow-saved-world-buxman-speaker-hall-of-fame/.

Lightening the mood offers both parties a chance to take a breath and maybe even retreat from earlier demands. Again, it works best with colleagues you've grown to know and trust.

Still, tread lightly when inserting humor into serious negotiations or heated conflicts. You don't want to be accused of being uncaring. Used properly, humor serves as a reminder that you do care. Even in that moment of conflict, you're on the same team. There's room for differing opinions. We're all doing our best.

There really isn't much room for sarcasm and mockery. Try a little self-deprecation instead. Even before negotiations get started, as introductions begin, someone is bound to say some form of, "How are you today?" I actually recommend you have a collection of answers to consider other than "Fine." See if any of these fit your style.

"Overworked and underpaid."

"So far, so good."

"Ask me in half an hour. It all depends on this meeting."

"Other than having a bad hair day, I'm fine."

"Wondering how you are."

"Kids are good. Wife loves me. Can't complain."

"Walking on sunshine."

Beyond the business world, humor should come naturally in families. And it's especially valuable in difficult times. For example, it's not uncommon for grieving siblings to find themselves in conflict at the reading of the parents' last will and testament. But if you can get your brothers and sisters reminiscing and eventually smiling about Mom's quirks and Dad's forgetfulness, then the day will go more smoothly. You won't get the estate changed, but you might leave the lawyer's office in better spirits.

Using humor to diffuse conflict comes with a few common-sense warnings. Poke fun at the problem, not any one person. Humor should suggest that you're all on the same page, that you understand each other. Jokes can lampoon the foibles of an industry, but should probably not disparage a particular individual or company. The final warning regarding humor is that forcing a joke into a serious situation can backfire. Make sure everyone involved knows you can be counted on in difficult times. After the negotiations, the last thing you want to be known as is a "clown."

In addition to sharing a laugh, there are other skills you can try in order to diffuse tension that can reboot any tense conversation. Talk about your pets. Come in whistling. Wear a bowtie. Bring donuts. Maybe go ahead and tell that knock-knock joke your kid told you earlier. Anything that's relatable. The goal is to remind all parties involved that we're not robots and that conflict requires a human touch.

GIVE KIDS A BREAK:
Conflict as a learning tool

This may seem like advice for parents, but anyone over thirty has certainly found themselves in a moment of potential conflict with a teenager, apprentice, rookie, or other newcomer.

That young person did something silly, boneheaded, illogical, or just plain wrong, and your first instinct is to come down hard on them. For example, you just finished telling them the paint is wet, but they have to test it themselves. You give clear instructions about a safety feature designed to keep them from cutting their fingers off, and they still almost cut their fingers off. For a recipe, you instruct them to use twice as much of some ingredient and they pull out their smartphone to do the multiplication.

Please don't scream, lecture, or give up on them. If you really need to, you can roll your eyes and later tell some of your mature friends about the young goofball you have on your hands. But really, youthful folly shouldn't come as a surprise.

Proverbs 22:15 confirms that God designed young people to sometimes push the limits of right and wrong: "Folly is bound up in the heart of a child." For the most part, a teenager or inexperienced twenty-something who contradicts common sense is not the kind of conflict that needs resolution. It's just young people being young people. We were all there at some point. (At least most of us.)

Another verse, Ecclesiastes 11:9 (NLT) even seems to give teenagers and young adults permission to go a little crazy. But make sure you read the entire verse: "Young people, it's wonderful to be young! Enjoy every minute of it. Do everything you want to do; take it all in. But remember that you must give an account to God for everything you do."

I take all of this to mean that God expects all of us to get into some mischief and make a mistake once in a while, especially when we're young. To be clear though, we're not getting away with anything. He will hold us accountable for our decisions and actions.

Think of it this way: Mistakes and impulsive decisions are part of God's design for young people's training. Valuable lessons can be learned without too much permanent damage. In many cases, the consequences when a young person acts impulsively are not quite as dire as bad decisions made by older folks. When you're young, broken bones heal faster; society is a little more forgiving of youthful indiscretions. Plus, there's time to put the past in the past. For example, if a young person loses their life savings to a con artist, the amount is minimal and there's time to start building a new nest egg from scratch.

If you find yourself in a management or mentoring relationship with a young person, consider it an opportunity to impact the future. God might even use you to refine and develop them. When coming alongside that blossoming young person—withholding judgment and minimizing your derision—you may be asked to give gentle correction and positive encouragement. Is that something you can do? Will you make yourself available?

By the way, in the process be open to learning some new lessons yourself. Young people aren't stupid. They're just not as savvy in the ways of the world. All that to say there's a high likelihood that young person knows stuff you don't.

SHINE LIGHT IN THE SHADOWS:
Bring the conflict out into the open

Before the next showdown—or maybe right in the middle of it—see if you can confront the issue head on. Right out loud, confess your frustration. Admit your own culpability in any ongoing feud. Find out if there's an underlying obstacle to the two of you working things out. Maybe just ask, "Are you okay? Is it something I've done?"

Admittedly, this strategy isn't easy and could backfire in many ways. Your adversary might just be a jerk. The ensuing confrontation may uncover irreconcilable differences. You may not care enough to put in that kind of effort. The nature of your organization may make that conversation impossible. Sometimes two decent people have a different viewpoint on what matters in life.

On the other hand, if somehow both of you open your hearts and maybe even spill your guts, you may learn something new and suddenly find yourselves to be compatible workmates. Or even friends. That might seem optimistic, but what if the ongoing enmity has been caused be a clear case of mistaken identity, miscommunication, or a rumor fabricated by some scheming third party? Maybe without knowing it, you inadvertently did something months ago that caused real harm to your adversary. You'd want to know about it, right?

You've seen enough sitcoms to know that conflict is often a direct result of something quite innocent that gets blown out of proportion. That happens in the friendliest workplace or the happiest home. Still, conflict can also come from one or both parties making bad decisions and refusing to admit any responsibility.

Bringing the conflict out into the light is almost always revealing. The essence of the conflict may be uncovered. Moreover, if your adversary continually lurks in the shadows it might be because they have something to hide. John 3:20 tells us, "For everyone who does wicked things hates the light and does not come to the light, lest his works should be exposed" (ESV).

MATCH THEIR EMOTIONS:
Get on the same side of any conflict

My junior year of high school, I was captain of the junior varsity (JV) wrestling team. Believe me, that is not impressive. By junior year, the goal is to crack the varsity starting squad. If you follow wrestling, you know that most teams have quite a few juniors, some sophomores, and even a freshman or two on varsity.

One Saturday late in the season, my team had an out-of-town JV tournament. My parents made it to most of my matches, but it was a long day and a long ride, so I didn't mind that they weren't in the stands that time. As it turns out, I took first place in my weight class.

At home, I showed the modest trophy to my father and waited for his response. He held it in his hand, looked at it thoughtfully, and said, "Maybe next year you can win a varsity trophy."

Until that point, it had been a good day. With eight wrestlers in my 138-pound bracket, I had come out on top. But my dad's remark cut me like a knife. Words from a parent can do that. But as harsh as his words sounded, they weren't inaccurate. The goal for a high school wrestler is to make the varsity lineup and rack up some wins at that level. You might even say those words needed to be said. *But not that day.* After the season or over the summer, there would be time to talk about my wrestling goals for senior year.

What should my dad have said as he held that trophy? "Wonderful! Sorry we missed it." "Tell me about that championship match." "You deserve this, I know how hard you've been working." Those kinds of responses unify relationships.

To be clear, there was no expectation on my part of a giant banner or a victory parade. After all, the local paper didn't even cover JV sports. But that moment was a time for modest celebration, and it would have been nice if my dad had, well, celebrated. In other words, a moment of emotion should be matched by the same emotion.

Do you want to have influence or gain partnership? Whatever your "adversary" is going through, see if you can mirror their emotions. Romans 12:15 says, "Rejoice with those who rejoice; mourn with those who mourn" (NIV).

So do that. Laugh with them. Cry with them. Celebrate with them. Maybe even get a little angry right alongside them. If your adversary is going through an emotion of any kind, it may be tempting to express the opposite. But that reaction will escalate any conflict you have with them.

Want to quickly get on the same side as your adversary? Match their emotions.

By the way, years later my father and I talked about that Saturday tournament and modest trophy. He recalled being quite proud, but admitted he was just doing what so many dads do. And rightfully so. He was challenging me to the next level.

DON'T JUST PAINT OVER IT:
Kill the conflict for keeps

Have you ever finished painting over water stains or crayon marks only to discover the blemishes are still visible? You think you're done. You put away the ladder, pull up the tarp, and wash the brushes and roller, but when the paint dries the discoloration on the wall or ceiling somehow magically appears more obvious than ever. Aggravating, isn't it?

Should have used Kilz. It's a pretty remarkable product. The manufacturer describes it as "a fast drying sealer that blocks most severe stains including tannin bleed, graffiti, smoke, fire and water stains as well as sealing pet, smoke, and food odors." In other words, using Kilz as a primer makes the problem go away forever. There are Kilz formulations that block mold, mildew, drywall dust, grease, tape residue, and even Sharpie markers.

The principle is simple and applies to most conflicts in life. Effective conflict resolution needs to acknowledge the root of the problem and offer a lasting solution. Otherwise the conflict just keeps coming back.

Marriage counselors confirm that reconciliation is impossible without engaging in honest communication that gets below the surface to reveal the source of the strife and the mutual benefits of staying together.

It's the same with parenting. When the twins are fighting, Mom or Dad might successfully get them to stop and shake hands. But when left alone, those two fourth graders go right back at it. Why? Because no one took the time to discern the underlying cause of the squabble. What's more, even that might not have been enough. The twins also need to be convinced of the benefits of protecting, defending, and loving each other.

On the job, just about all of us will find ourselves—for perhaps unknown reasons—constantly butting heads with one specific coworker. When that happens, we can expend a lot of effort avoiding that person, chronicling their shortcomings, plotting revenge, or undermining their work. But wouldn't it be more productive to see what's at the root of the contention? That's easier said than done, but it's within your power.

This book is filled with strategies, ideas, advice, angles, and mandates to get to the root of your next or ongoing conflict. Consider this chapter a reminder to take that challenge all the way to its logical conclusion. Don't just paint over it. Because if that's all you do, before long it will almost always come back worse than any mold, mildew, graffiti, or grease stain you can imagine.

RECOGNIZE THE BARRIERS TO RECONCILIATION:
Discern your own part in the conflict

Expanding on the theme of the last short scenario—resolving a conflict permanently—let's talk about reoccurring conflicts. They might be the result of one particular adversary turning out to be a repeat offender. For unknown reasons, there will always be one or two people in life who rub you the wrong way.

When they show up, trouble ensues. By the way, the feeling might be mutual.

Or it could be some circumstance that keeps coming back just when you thought you had vanquished it for good. Like a rash that reappears just in time for swimsuit season.

If one persistent conflict becomes your thorn in the flesh, maybe it's time to do whatever it takes to make it go away. Permanently. Other than hiring a hitman, your best choice might be to go to the person and keep talking until you uncover the real source of the problem. When it comes to interpersonal conflict these days, respectful and nonjudgmental conversations seem to be in short supply. But as we've already established, the pathway to de-escalation quite often requires a heartfelt (or at least an honest) dialogue to reveal any stubborn barrier to reconciliation.

Let's list some possibilities. First, as previously stated, it could be a simple case of miscommunication. That should be easy enough to figure out. Put all your cards on the table and that just might prompt your adversary to do the same. A long-ago inadvertent snub or some other misunderstanding could easily cause a stalemate between two otherwise easygoing and even-tempered adversaries.

However, it may be deeper than that. You may be dealing with issues that require some forthright assessment to determine the source of conflict. It could be an emotional barrier including envy, insecurity, lack of trust, self-contempt, loneliness, shame, or pride. It could be situational or environmental differences which include finances, age, marital status, birth order, cultural differences, business experience, family history, job responsibilities, or simply a different set of expectations you bring to the relationship.

Let's also remember there are two sides to every conflict.

As you read that list of emotional or situational barriers you were likely discerning which of those troublesome flaws might be embedded in the personality of your adversary. But hold on now! As humans we never think we're the problem. That's why—if we experience a reoccurring conflict—it's a good idea to turn that mirror on ourselves and see who we really are. Maybe it's our own envy or pride causing the conflict. Maybe after being on the job for decades we've forgotten what it's like to be a rookie. Maybe you and your adversary were raised in different cultures with differing priorities. Maybe it's time you walked a mile in your adversary's shoes. Or put another way, what if you tried "carrying each other's burdens"?

> Carry each other's burdens, and in this way you will fulfill the law of Christ. If anyone thinks they are something when they are not, they deceive themselves. Each one should test their own actions. Then they can take pride in themselves alone, without comparing themselves to someone else, for each one should carry their own load. (Galatians 6:2–5)

If it's a temporary relationship—sitting next to someone on a plane, sharing a dorm room for a weekend, or being assigned to a project for a month—then uncovering the root cause of your aversion or animosity is totally optional. But if you're going to be living, working, or volunteering alongside this person for any length of time, then do the right thing.

Test yourself. If you realize you may have been contributing to the conflict, then try a new approach. Carry your own load. And maybe take some of that burden off your adversary.

ONE-ON-ONE RECONCILIATION:
When sin puts you in conflict with another believer

This Skill to Build is not easy. It takes empathy, discernment, humility, and courage to follow the instructions in Matthew 18, which explains how to confront someone who you believe has sinned against you. Read these three verses a couple times.

> If another believer sins against you, go privately and point out the offense. If the other person listens and confesses it, you have won that person back. But if you are unsuccessful, take one or two others with you and go back again, so that everything you say may be confirmed by two or three witnesses. If the person still refuses to listen, take your case to the church. Then if he or she won't accept the church's decision, treat that person as a pagan or a corrupt tax collector. (Matthew 18:15–17 NLT)

Can you visualize the steps laid out here? First you need to be very clear about identifying and confirming that some kind of sin has taken place. That cannot be about your own sense of righteousness. It's about knowing and applying a biblical standard of right and wrong, and only applies to a brother or sister in Christ.

Second, this process needs to occur under strict confidentiality.

Then you'll want to find a time and a place for you and that brother or sister to talk. To be clear, you're about to point out some area of their life in which they may be sinning. You cannot take that lightly, and you know they won't either. Begin by affirming your relationship. Whatever you need to say, express it with a gentle spirit. Begin by making observations rather than accusations.

Per the instructions in Matthew, try to win them over, and be quick to help them find forgiveness. God's grace should come easily. Then, offer your own forgiveness and help them to forgive themselves.

Beyond that first meeting, if there's pushback or the dispute deepens, you have a decision to make. Without ganging up on that brother or sister, you may want to get others involved, including a pastor or elders—then perhaps an entire church community. If your accusation cannot be backed up by witnesses, then, rightfully so, the matter should probably be dropped. Worst-case scenario: if and when evidence substantiates the unrepentant sin, your relationship may need to be severed.

Oddly, this exercise is not about creating harmony. Applying the "Matthew 18 Principle" is about restoring integrity. Even successfully applied, there may still be hard feelings or reparations to be made.

As described in this passage from the Gospel of Matthew, this interaction takes courage and follow-through from both parties. Over the years, I've both received and given this kind of admonishment a few times. When both parties come to the interaction with respect and empathy, it's an effective strategy. The sin is acknowledged, and the matter doesn't have to advance beyond that first honest advisement.

Full disclosure: I must confess that on at least two occasions a Christian friend pointed out one of my own shortcomings, and I did not receive it well. My response—a half-hearted apology—did forestall the matter from escalating, so their courageous observations had value. In the process, I even gained some personal insight. But those relationships never healed completely. Take that as a caution and a reminder that all of us are flawed humans.

SKIP REVENGE:
Respond to conflict with kindness

Yes, I know it would feel great to flip a switch and watch your adversary go down in flames. Especially if they've intentionally been a chronic pain in your backside. But that's a feeling you need to rise above. When we make business or life decisions based on revenge, we often end up losing money, burning bridges, making fools of ourselves, feeling regret, or hurting our own interests more than theirs.

Revenge is like throwing a hot coal at someone else—we burn our own hand more than the person we are trying to hurt. The Bible has a better plan. You're still delivering that hot coal, but in an unexpected way. It may seem counterintuitive, but try doing everything within reason to meet their physical, financial, and emotional needs. Romans 12:20 says, "If your enemy is hungry, feed him; if he is thirsty, give him something to drink; for by so doing you will heap burning coals on his head" (ESV).

The imagery should almost make you chuckle. By choosing to meet the needs of your persecutors, your actions may shine light into their dark hearts for the very first time. Your generosity, reluctant though it is, may open their eyes to how they've been acting and the damage they've done. There's a good chance they have wronged others as well, leaving a trail of enemies along the way.

Suddenly you come along and treat them with love and respect. Your display of grace will get their attention. (Almost as if you've dumped hot coals on their heads!) You might even say you're killing them with kindness. That strategy works in all facets of life, not just the workplace.

What's more, grudges rarely bring satisfaction. You may have their attention, but please don't expect an apology. If you're holding a grudge or contemplating revenge, you're actually suffering while the person who did you wrong feels no pain. The late, great comedian Buddy Hackett had some valuable insight on the subject: "I've had a few arguments with people, but I never carry a grudge. You know why? While you're carrying a grudge, they're out dancing."

But the best reason to skip revenge is the long-term positive impact that choice can have on future interactions with this particular adversary and others. As you know, word gets around—in business and life. You might imagine that having a reputation as a ruthless negotiator who takes no prisoners would serve you well. But just think about it. Next time you're considering a new supplier, customer, or partner, would you pursue a relationship with someone who has a reputation for being relentless and iron-fisted, or someone who plays nice?

Said another way: reputation matters.

TERMINATE TOXICITY:
When conflict is part of their DNA

An ongoing theme in this book is optimism. I hope you're seeing how there can be great value in conflict. It can even lead to new creativity, productivity, friendships, and much-needed conversations. What's more, I believe most people want to reduce negative conflict in their lives. Fewer screaming matches. Less walking on eggshells. More cooperation. More empathy.

But there are people out there—and you know a few—who seem to thrive on divisiveness. When they enter the room or Zoom call, you know they'll soon be stirring up trouble. At Thanksgiving, they're dragging up issues that every other family member has put in the past. It could be a beautiful spring day, but this neighbor is pointing out your dandelions or cracked concrete, or spreading gossip or whining about garbage pickup.

On the job, they may be intelligent and effective, but they make everyone else feel cruddy and distract from overall productivity. You could label it verbal or emotional abuse.

Sometimes it's overtly and obviously malicious. Sometimes you don't realize what's happening until later. After spending just fifteen minutes with that individual, you feel inadequate, angry, or disheartened. Who needs that?

After you realize what's going on, you start spending way too much time and energy avoiding these toxic folks. Changing your routine. Making excuses. Coming up with exit strategies for when they corner you in some toxic conversation. That can be so exhausting, not to mention unproductive.

Even worse, sometimes you find yourself joining the avalanche of negativity or becoming part of the drama.

What to do? Some therapists, lifestyle bloggers, and newspaper advice columnists say, "Cut them out of your life." That actually might be a good idea, especially if they're not a significant part of your life. Stop going to the shop, gym, or salon where they work or hang out. If they're second cousins, maybe you no longer have room at the holiday table. If they live five houses away, change your walking route. Don't pick up when you see their name on caller ID. Literally stop interacting with them.

But what if they live right next door, married your brother, work in your four-person office, are one of your most profitable customers, or simply cannot be cut out of your life? Then—no surprise—you have to double down on the skill of de-escalation. Try these strategies.

- First and foremost, protect yourself. Physically and emotionally.
- Establish boundaries.

- Never join them in their pity party or negative trash talk.
- Be "too busy" or "on deadline" or "heading out the door."
- Counter toxicity with over-the-top cheerfulness and hope.
- Counter toxicity with corrections based on fact.
- Ignore insults by mentally and emotionally devaluing the source.
- Soften their hurtful words by surrounding yourself with positive influences.
- See the absurdity or humor in their words or actions.
- Finally, if they become abusive, don't let them get away with it. Maybe even get in their face.

Don't start a battle you can't win. But if there's a chance you can actually talk them into a new reality, then go for it. Maybe they don't realize how toxic they are. Or maybe it's a cry for help, and God has assigned you to be a difference maker. Is it possible your enthusiastic positivity and new skills of de-escalation can make a real difference in their life and all their relationships?

Oops. There I go again being optimistic.

KNOW THINE ENEMY:
Championing conflict

Hopefully, we've successfully established that conflict does more than reflect the baser human instincts—primeval, animalistic—requiring us to get down and dirty. It does not always result in hardship or affliction.

You may even be able to shrug your shoulders and think, *I guess conflict is neutral. Sometimes good, sometimes bad.* Based on previous chapters and your own life experience, that seems like a reasonable conclusion.

Dare we take it a step further, even *championing* conflict? Can we suggest that conflict has life-giving, redeeming value for all mankind?

Allow me to submit that conflict is actually the building block of humanity and culture. We are all better because of it. A brief overview of the arts bears witness to a wide range of examples which make that case.

Painters imbue their work with a conflict between light and dark. Composers weave crescendos with decrescendos of clashing strings, brass, woodwinds, and percussion. Dance attempts to defy gravity. Theatre doesn't exist without conflict, usually between main characters.

Any serious student of literature recognizes the concept of a narrative arc and how it encompasses at least one of the six types of conflict.

Person vs. Person: Think Sherlock Holmes matching wits with Professor Moriarty. Or Sam-I-Am refusing to sample the narrator's green breakfast.

Person vs. Self: Hamlet famously asks himself, "To be or not to be?"

Person vs. Nature: Classic examples are Herman Melville's *Moby Dick* and Ernest Hemingway's *The Old Man and the Sea*.

Person vs. Society: In *The Scarlet Letter,* Nathaniel Hawthorne cast Hester Prynne as an adulterer shunned by her Puritan community. George Orwell visits this theme in *Animal Farm* and *1984*.

Person vs. Technology: Paul Bunyan vs. the steam-powered saw is an early example in folklore. This is, of course, a common trope in science fiction.

Person vs. the Supernatural: Greek literature is filled with man doing battle with the gods. Tolkien's *Lord of the Rings* trilogy features Frodo and his hobbit friends in a supernatural battle with the Dark Lord Sauron. Any time a fictional character wrestles with right and wrong might be considered an example of Person vs. God.

A single piece of literature can include several layers and examples of conflict. In the opening chapters of the 1862 novel *Les Misérables*, Jean Valjean finds himself with a bundle of stolen candlesticks, which leads to a transformational reconciliation with God. His ongoing conflict with Inspector Javert reflects Person vs. Person. In the 1985 musical, the song, "Who Am I?" clearly reflects an internal battle of Person vs. Self. Valjean's relationship with God comes full circle in the afterlife found in the final scene.

To an artist, conflict is a tool. Something that creates a dilemma for the novel to resolve. A knot for the play to untangle. A void for the music to fill.

If the arts champion conflict, what value is that to you and me? Beyond bringing beauty and stirring our imaginations, we are reminded that the great lessons—the great turning points in life—are often the direct result of conflict. Untold friendships, partnerships, and strong marriages have been forged in such moments.

In the bigger picture of the many conflicts in our own lives, this idea points to a skill certainly worth building. That is, the ability to identify an adversary and see an opportunity instead of an enemy.

CHAPTER 7

TACTICS AND TRICKS

You may have opened this book, skimmed the table of contents, and turned right to this section first. I completely understand. You're in a conflict right now, and you need to come out on top. You agree there's value in determining priorities, assessing risks, considering case studies, and applying Scripture. You also know you have skills to polish regarding communication, problem-solving, and even how you see conflict.

But you're willing to set that aside. You're in urgent need of negotiation tricks and shrewd tactics you can use right now, today.

Okay then. You are allowed full access to these thirteen tactics and tricks, but only if you promise to use them for good, not for evil. Deal?

Call in a Favor

One of the advantages of being a basically good person is that you've stored up some goodwill. You've gone the extra mile on difficult projects. You stepped up when no one else volunteered. During the worst of the COVID pandemic, you remained optimistic and rallied the team. You sat with grandma in the hospital. When someone needs a hand or listening ear, they know you're the kind of person who'll drop everything to give them your full attention. You're a person of integrity, faith, and honor.

If that's your reputation, maybe it's time to cash in. This is really hard for some people to do. But see if you can find a moment of calm in the conflict, gain the full attention of your adversary, and speak earnestly and candidly on your own behalf:

"I know we're on opposite sides of this problem, but I'm going to ask this one time if I can take the lead on this. Can you let me do that?"

"I have to say, I feel so strongly about this. I understand what you're saying. But, really, I'm simply asking you to trust me on this. Okay?"

"You know how much I value our family (or this company/ church/community). Just the fact that I am taking this stand—putting our relationship in jeopardy—should tell you how important this decision is to me. Please, for everyone's sake, can we try it my way?"

Finish your sincere request in the form of a question, then stay silent. Let that question hang in the air for a while. Don't stare the other person down, but do make brief eye contact. You have put them in charge, and their response will tell you how to proceed. They may smile, shake their head, and say, "Okay, you win." Or they may say, "Nope, sorry." But at least you'll know, and you can move on to some other approach.

Of course, if calling in a favor works, you can't use it again for a while.

Play Hardball

Almost the opposite of calling in a favor is the idea of refusing to acknowledge any friendship, personal equity, and past relationships during negotiations. This strategy requires you to clearly verbalize your demands and your walk-away points early on—leaving no room for give and take. Drawing those hard lines is risky territory, because you may win the battle but lose the war.

The only way to make playing hardball work is to have a personal conviction about those specific demands and then verbally admit what you're doing.

"Joshua, I know we go way back. Most of the time, I have some wiggle room when we're working out details, but this time is different. Here's what I need..."

You can only make this unequivocal demand if you have an ongoing, high-integrity relationship. What's more, if you want to keep that relationship, you can't play hardball all the time.

Pass the Buck

Sometimes the most efficient way to negotiate is to confess that you can't. In truth, you may have all kinds of power. The buck may stop with you. But if you're offering a fair deal and you don't have the time to mess around, the best idea might be to say something like, "I am authorized today to make this offer. Take it or leave it. Anything else might take weeks or months."

This is a version of playing hardball that suggests your best offer is actually out of your hands. You're no longer the tough-talking opposition; you're simply delivering a message from upstairs.

Passing the buck works especially well with relationships that only last through a single negotiation.

Make the First Offer

Whether you're the buyer or the seller, someone has to make the first offer. You can usually assume that when the deal is ultimately done, the final number will be remarkably close to that original offer. Which means if your adversary makes the first offer, you need to be prepared to live with that. Or something close to it.

If you've done your homework and know what the market will allow, go ahead and speak first, and don't be afraid of being a bit more aggressive than feels comfortable. You don't want to be insulting with your offer. But you also don't want to cheat yourself.

If you're selling or buying a product, industry standards should help you decide what to charge or offer to pay based on the cost of manufacturing. But if you're negotiating on a service—which is more about time and expertise—it's much more difficult for you and your adversary to know what's fair. Speak first and read their response. You can backtrack if necessary, but don't be surprised if your overall profitability increases measurably when you consistently make the first offer.

Ask a Favor

This strategy, known as "The Ben Franklin Effect," is designed to establish a long-term relationship with an adversary.[1] As the story goes, Benjamin Franklin once wanted to gain influence over a rival he knew was a book lover. The man was surprised when Franklin asked to borrow a rare book, but still he honored the request. Franklin thanked him graciously, kept the book about a week, and returned it in pristine condition, heaping on even more sincere gratitude. The man who had never wanted to speak to him before would become a dear friend for life. To quote Franklin: "He that has once done you a kindness will be more ready to do you another than he whom you yourself have obliged."

Interrupt the Pattern

Some conflicts show up again and again—either from the same adversary or difficult situations that tend to repeat themselves. If past experience tells you conflict is coming, develop a strategy to interrupt that conflict before it happens.

One example is the coworker who repeatedly takes sole credit for ideas that were, in actuality, a group effort. Everyone who contributed knows that coworker's pattern of credit-grabbing needs to stop. The best time and place to interrupt the pattern is at the beginning of the presentation of the idea. With the appropriate parties gathered in the room or video conference, take the floor and make

---

[1] Jonathan Becher, "Do Me a Favor So You'll Like Me: The Reverse Psychology of Likeability," *Forbes*, November 16, 2011, https://www.forbes.com/sites/sap/2011/11/16/do-me-a-favor-so-youll-like-me-the-reverse-psychology-of-likeability/?sh=214aa09c74a5.

a big deal about how rewarding it was to be part of a team that works together so well. Message delivered.

Speaking of patterns, let's talk about wallpaper. If you're one of the homeowners who still hangs wallpaper from time to time, you are dreading the redecorating project you and your spouse have been planning for months. You know it will leave you screaming at each other for an entire weekend. Every time you wallpaper together you pledge to never do it again. So instead, as an anniversary gift to each other, hire a professional. Conflict avoided.

Traffic cops also see patterns when they pull someone over for speeding. It's typically miffed drivers with bad attitudes denying their guilt or making lame excuses. So interrupt that pattern. Be respectful. Admit you were speeding. Then simply ask, "Is there any way you can give me a warning ticket?" A carinsurance.com survey indicated that strategy worked for drivers 41 percent of the time.[2]

A friend of mine who used to drive a taxi told me that occasionally, inebriated passengers would dash from his cab without paying. More than once, he had to jump out and chase them down. Eventually, he began to sense when a fare was likely to pull that trick. When he picked up that vibe, he would playfully tap his brakes and jerk his steering wheel as he drove. The startled passengers would respond: "Hey! What are you doing!"

"Oh just making sure we get you home safe and sound," my friend might reply, initiating a conversation. By interrupting the pattern, he humanized himself, coming across as more than a cab

---

[2] Jonathan Becher, "Do Me a Favor So You'll Like Me: The Reverse Psychology of Likeability," *Forbes*, November 16, 2011, https://www.forbes.com/sites/sap/2011/11/16/do-me-a-favor-so-youll-like-me-the-reverse-psychology-of-likeability/?sh=214aa09c74a5.

driver. Upon reaching the final destination, the rider would pay the full fare plus a nice tip.

If you know a conflict is looming, think to yourself, *How can I interrupt the pattern? How can I stop the conflict before it starts?*

Tit for Tat

This tactic is all about making today's conflict go away and maybe preventing the next one. It may be difficult for some because it requires them to stand up to intimidation.

Bullies initiate conflict because they know they will almost always come out way ahead. Don't let them. Steel yourself against threats and scare tactics. When conflict becomes coercion, you need to go tit for tat. Make it a transaction. If you give an inch, insist they do the same. Stand your ground as long as you can.

A good example of going "tit for tat" is standing up to school-yard bullies. Remember the raccoon-hat wearing character of Scut Farkus in the 1983 film *A Christmas Story*? He lived to pick on Ralphie, but when Ralphie finally had enough and came out swinging, Farkus got his own bloody nose. The conflict did escalate, but Farkus's bullying days were over.

By going "tit for tat," you'll break even in the first round—and next time your adversary has two choices. They will find an easier victim or treat you fairly, knowing you can't be taken advantage of.

Kill Your Darlings

This term refers to a painful but necessary editing practice. Sometimes fiction writers have to cut a storyline, passage, or even an entire character out of the narrative. Successful authors know anything that is overly cute, clichéd, unnecessary, or overblown needs to go—even if that means cutting a darling paragraph or chapter they have spent hours polishing. Killing your darlings means letting go of stuff you like which isn't important to your end goals.

Applied to conflict resolution, that can give you a significant edge. Examples?

- Dividing up the family estate, all your relatives know you loved Grandpa's mahogany desk. By letting Cousin Horatio have it, you are more likely to get other stuff.
- You could argue with the coach about batting cleanup, but surrendering that coveted spot in the lineup may best serve the team and cement your role as a leader.
- An architectural firm can argue all they want about the value of photovoltaic panels and capturing rainwater, but if the developer doesn't care about green design, they'll need to "kill those darlings" if they hope to get the bid.

Change Minds via Social Media

Don't bother. It can't be done.

In the early days, the great online social media community was promoted as a way to gather in harmony to share ideas and gain a better understanding of each other. It didn't last.

Unfortunately, today we meet in silos. We're only hearing and listening to people who already believe what we believe. We block those who disagree with us. As a result, we eliminate any chance of empathy, which is one of the primary factors in de-escalating conflict.

As proof, just consider what happens when a stance or policy that has clear consensus in one silo somehow finds its way into an opposing silo. That sound bite, quote, clip, or meme is labeled as hate speech and goes viral. Instead of changing minds, the conflict escalates.

To reiterate: Attempting to change minds via social media is not a recommended tactic or trick. It's a waste of time.

Speak Last

A lot of negotiators, speechmakers, and delegates seem to like the sound of their own voice. When an issue comes up for debate at a forum, council, school board, or policy meeting, they speak first, long, and loud. The strategy of speaking first can fail for several reasons.

First, the audience or decision makers are typically just getting settled in, and the key points of the controversy have not even been identified. Second, those in attendance are either preparing their own speaking notes or still discerning their own goals. Third, the longer your adversary speaks—as you use your active listening skills—the more ammunition you have to use their own words against them. Fourth, as the debate progresses, the specific points of those who spoke early are long forgotten. Finally, those who choose to speak last have a chance to take notes, think through their responses, and effectively summarize the entire meeting. But here's the sneaky part. They're not shooting down arguments. They invest the first part of their platform time agreeing with all the points that seemed to hit the mark with the decision makers. Then with just a little spin, they can clearly state why their proposal is the best-case scenario for meeting the needs of everyone in attendance. Speaking last arms you with the most recent information from the widest range of sources.

Science also supports the benefits in setting yourself up to be one of the final speakers. The "recency effect" is a popular theory in cognitive psychology, suggesting that when presented with a list of options or ideas, individuals are most likely to recall whatever they heard last.

Avoid the Quick Correction

Instantly correcting a false statement by an adversary may feel good, but it's usually not a good idea. Even if you're right, you've stirred an even deeper emotion in your adversary, which may cause them to more deeply entrench in their battle against you. What's more, there are other, more effective strategies for coming out ahead in the debate or conflict.

If their false statement is an unequivocal factual error, simply make note of it and wait. Very likely, the truth will eventually come out and the speaker will stand corrected. If their untruth goes unchallenged and is about to impact a decision being made today, then find a way to bring it up gently and judiciously. Something like, "A point of order. There was some discussion earlier suggesting titanium would be less expensive, but my notes say that stainless steel is about 20 percent cheaper." Remember to keep your long-term goal in mind, which is to make the right choice, not to make your adversary look bad.

Another way to turn a disagreement around without verbally bludgeoning a speaker is to use a debate technique known as the Ransberger Pivot, first described in 1982 by Ray Ransberger and Marshall Fritz.[3] The three-part methodology changes the framework

---

[3] David Galloway, "Is Arguing Ever Productive?" Continuous Mile, December 1, 2014, https://www.continuousmile.com/behavior/arguing-words-matter/.

of a conflict by putting opposing parties on the same side. Instead of attacking your adversary, you strategically find common ground and advance the conversation as peers. It begins with respectful listening and, perhaps, asking open-ended questions such as, "Why do you feel that way?" Continue listening until you find a position of common ground that you can articulate. "That's exactly right…" "I think we're on the same page here…" "You've hit on something that's also important to me…" After you listen and validate their position, then you can explain why your position is a viable solution to your mutual concern.

The point here is that saying, "You're wrong!" is almost always a dead end to any kind of mutually beneficial agreement. Helping your adversary "save face" is the way to go.

Yield Unexpectedly

Heading into a debate or conflict, if you know your adversary's specific demands, surprise him by unexpectedly giving in. While he celebrates the victory, present your own demands or expectations.

For example, a buyer lowballs an offer for ten thousand widgets. You say yes! But then tell them you're filling the order with last year's model. (Which you've been trying to unload anyway.)

Your contractor informs you the kitchen remodel is going to be an extra $1,200. You say okay—but only if it's completed by the deadline you've been hoping they will hit all along.

Your girlfriend drops not-so-subtle hints for an engagement ring. You say yes! But then set a date far, far off in the future.

Actually, I'm not 100 percent sure that last example is a good idea, but you get the point. Like so many conflict resolutions, it's all about timing and expectations. Sometimes you do have to give in so you can get what you really want.

Be Human

There are plenty of ruthless, cold-blooded, callous tormentors out there. You'll find them down dark alleys, in boardrooms, on college campuses, and at city council meetings—sometimes even in church pews and the best of families. But most people—even those with whom you have conflict—are not heartless. Which means you can't go wrong presenting your own human side, especially if your adversary doesn't know much about you.

Early in your meeting, before the nitty-gritty of negotiations or debate, spend a moment making a personal connection. Talking about weather or traffic is safe, but tiresome. If possible, do a bit of research ahead of time to size up your adversary. See if you can connect on a real-life level. Mention a household project, a new hobby you've been enjoying, or even a song going through your head. If it feels right, shake your head and mention how your kids' busy schedule is driving you crazy. You're not bragging and you're not looking for sympathy, but maybe they can relate with their own stories. If you can get your adversary talking about themselves, you are halfway to winning them over. If they pull out their phone and show you recent pics of their kids, grandkids, or cats, any conflict is practically off the table.

This is not a con; you're sincerely looking to make a friend, because friends treat friends fairly. And, who knows, you might make a new one.

CHAPTER 8

A WAY OF LIFE

I understand most readers did not pick up this book looking for a new way of life. They were already doing well and didn't consider themselves to be in the market for a major overhaul. They just wanted a bit of help in dealing with some of life's conflicts.

After plowing through the first seven sections, you might be good to go. You're ready and eager to begin de-escalating conflicts in every area of your life. You have efficiently mastered the Four Factors, polished your Skills to Build, and uncovered a few useful Tactics and Tricks. That's all good news.

What's more, when the previous chapters referenced biblical principles, you were 100 percent on board. After all, lots of self-help books quote from the Bible. Plus, who doesn't want God on their side? But that doesn't mean a "new way of life" is anywhere on your shopping list.

If that's the case, feel free to close this book and enthusiastically put into practice your newly acquired strategies. Like all of us, you've got conflicts to overcome and adversaries to dominate.

However, if you keep reading you're likely to pick up on some principles not found in any other books on how to resolve conflicts in your favor.

Don't misunderstand: Bringing favorable conclusions to disputes and negotiations is still a worthy goal. Coming out of any conflict with a win is a beautiful thing. But is it possible that your definition of winning doesn't match up with God's?

In these final pages, I'll attempt to answer two questions about conflict that seem to keep coming up:

1. *After all the strategizing and maneuvering, why does it still feel like winning first prize is never enough?*

2. *With all the turmoil already in the world, when—if ever—should I initiate conflict?*

Thanks for sticking around to explore some answers. I promise you'll be glad you did.

ON BEING FIRST

One of the most amusing scenes in the Bible takes place on the road between Galilee and Capernaum. While walking along behind Jesus, all twelve disciples are engaged in an all-encompassing conflict, having the same debate humans have been obsessing over since time began.

They are arguing about which of them is the greatest. It's the classic obsession with being first. You can label it ambition, pride, self-importance, ego, the need to win at all costs, or even just an attempt to cement your legacy.

Striving to be your best self is not a bad thing, unless it distracts you from something more important. That's exactly what was happening in that historic scene recorded in Mark 9. You see, as they were walking, Jesus was sharing some pretty amazing stuff, even describing His upcoming betrayal, death, and resurrection. These were events Jesus's posse really needed to know, anticipate, and understand. But they weren't even listening.

When they arrived at Capernaum, finally He got their full attention. Of course, Jesus already knew their every thought; yet still He asked, "What were you arguing about on the road?" (v. 33) They got real quiet. They were embarrassed. Then Jesus delivered this stunner: "Anyone who wants to be first must be the very last, and the servant of all" (v. 35).

At that point the twelve probably turned from embarrassed to confused. *What does that mean? How can last be first?*

Maybe you can relate. You've spent your entire adult life working, studying, hustling, and successfully outmaneuvering your opponents. You are well aware of the world's definition of success: it's all about being first. First to reach the mountaintop. First at the box office. First in rushing yards or home runs. First place in whatever race you're running.

Often, you've even achieved that lofty goal and there was, indeed, a feeling of euphoria—for a short while. But it didn't last. As a matter of fact, a new yearning for the next big thing somehow took over alarmingly quickly.

That's when someone as sharp and astute as you begins to realize that maybe your definition of first place isn't quite accurate. That's also when the message Jesus delivered several times starts to make sense: "The last will be first, and the first will be last" (Matthew 20:16, Mark 10:31, Luke 13:30).

So what's going on? As creation reveals, God's standards are beyond our imagination. His ways are not our ways. When pondering the nature of the Creator, revelations and reversals should not come as surprises! The closer we get to Him, the more we will understand. But as soon as we start thinking we've got it all figured out or we're better than everyone else, we should expect to get taken down a notch or two.

Going back to Jesus's stunning statement to the apostles, we realize the answer is right there. In order to be first, we need to be "the servant of all." Hmmm. How do you do that?

First, start with a dose of humility. Second, take an honest inventory of your gifts. Not so you can boast about them, but to assess ways you can serve. Third, ask God to open your eyes to the needs of others. And that means everyone—from best friends to worst enemies—because the command is to be the "servant of all." Fourth, serve with love—not out of compulsion, guilt, or expectation of something in return. We can love because God first loved us.

The idea may sound impossible, even burdensome. But really, developing the heart of a servant requires a simple attitude adjustment. "In humility value others above yourselves, not looking to your own interests but each of you to the interests of the others" (Philippians 2:3–4).

I know that's not an idea you typically expect to read in a self-help book. More often you find something a little more, "Rah-rah! You can do it! Go! Fight! Win!" But that attitude works here, too. This servanthood concept is exciting stuff. World-changing, even. It's a message the world needs to hear.

In Capernaum, the apostles probably still didn't get that message. That's why Jesus later needed to give a practical lesson on serving at the Last Supper when He, the Son of God, washed their dusty feet and then told them, "I have set you an example that you should do as I have done for you" (John 13:15).

The apostles eventually understood. Jesus the Servant King made sure of that. Serving others is how the last becomes first. It's how you earn the King's inheritance. It's how you follow Jesus's example.

That's the secret to making an empty life full. And the secret to winning every face-off with any adversary. In your transactions or conflicts, find a way to serve.

Remember the first of the Four Factors? It's not "Decide what you want." It's "Decide what you really want." And what you really want should be finding your purpose beyond yourself and your own desires.

The acclaimed eighteenth-century preacher John Wesley expressed the same idea with this challenge:

Do all the good you can,
By all the means you can,
In all the ways you can,
In all the places you can,
At all the times you can,
To all the people you can,
As long as ever you can.

Wesley's list may be the formula for true greatness. Yes, we should absolutely strive for excellence. But God wants you to use your gifts and give best efforts to others ahead of yourself. Actually, put *everyone* ahead of yourself—which makes you last. But that's okay, because in God's economy that puts you back in first place, right where you belong.

ON CHOOSING CONFLICT

Should we ever choose conflict? Does any situation ever require a healthy dose of it?

The obvious answer is to point to the vivid scene described in all four gospels, in which Jesus displayed a powerful dose of righteous anger when He saw the religious leaders had turned God's house of worship into a place of extortion and profiteering. Jesus, the Prince of Peace, did not hesitate to create conflict when He saw earthly injustice.

> On reaching Jerusalem, Jesus entered the temple courts and began driving out those who were buying and selling there. He overturned the tables of the money changers and the benches of those selling doves, and would not allow anyone to carry merchandise through the temple courts. And as he taught them, he said, "Is it not written: 'My house will be called a house of prayer for all nations'? But you have made it 'a den of robbers.'" The chief priests and the teachers of the law heard this and began looking for a way to kill him, for they feared him, because the whole crowd was amazed at his teaching. (Mark 11:15–18)

Don't miss this point. Jesus's response to the desecration of the Temple had repercussions. Overturning the tables of the money changers could be considered the first act in the chain of events that led to His arrest, trial, and crucifixion. To be clear, none of this came as a surprise to Jesus. He stormed into the temple courts knowing he would face severe judgment and punishment. In this instance, Jesus chose not to "turn the other cheek." Most of the citizens of Jerusalem had probably grown to accept that the Temple became a marketplace every Passover. But Jesus *chose* conflict.

If someone asks you, "Is anger ever okay?" feel free to point to Jesus's righteous anger toward the money changers. But don't stop there. It's valuable to articulate that Jesus's *entire existence* was a point of conflict. When God becomes flesh, there's bound to be a disturbance in the normal routine of life. And it cannot be ignored.

As it turns out, Jesus offended many during His earthly ministry. Even today, following Him and quoting Him outside the walls of a church is considered inappropriate and offensive. Jesus Himself confirmed over and over that the Gospel is divisive.

> Do not suppose that I have come to bring peace to the earth. I did not come to bring peace, but a sword. For I have come to turn
> "a man against his father,
> a daughter against her mother,
> a daughter-in-law against her mother-in-law—
> a man's enemies will be the members of his own household."
> Anyone who loves his father or mother more than me is not worthy of me; anyone who loves his son or daughter more than me is not worthy of me; and anyone who does not take his cross and follow me is not worthy of me. (Matthew 10:34–38)

I hope that all makes sense. And I also hope you recognize the ultimate conundrum that Jesus did not come to bring some kind of temporary peace to this world; He came to do battle. To vanquish Satan. To bring light to the darkness. Jesus does promise peace, but it is accessible only to individuals who trust Him and call on His name. That decision may separate you from those you love, but ultimately Christ delivers peace, purpose, and satisfaction not available through worldly pursuits.

The conundrum is unraveled in John 14:27: "Peace I leave with you; my peace I give you. I do not give to you as the world gives. Do not let your hearts be troubled and do not be afraid."

Friend, if you've been hoping this book would help put an end to the conflict in your life, ultimately to claim some kind of peace, I would instead point you toward the Bible and Jesus Himself. There's a reason He is called the "Prince of Peace."

■   ■   ■

As for the immediate value of this book, I trust it has delivered a few practical strategies for dealing with matters of conflict in this world.

My goal was to arm you with some new business savvy, a bit of research, biblical truth, common sense, a few doses of encouragement, and some lessons learned the hard way.

Consider yourself equipped to face your next vexing conflict or worthy adversary with this thought:

"I choose not to run from this conflict, but I also choose *not to take the bait to escalate.*"